T0277701

# Hölderlin's Madness

SEAGULL
BOOKS
•
CELEBRATING
40 YEARS

THE ITALIAN LIST

**1.** Portrait of Hölderlin, age sixteen

GIORGIO AGAMBEN

*Hölderlin's Madness*

*Chronicle of a Dwelling Life*
*1806–1843*

TRANSLATED BY ALTA L. PRICE

LONDON NEW YORK CALCUTTA

The Italian List
*Series Editor*: Alberto Toscano

**Seagull Books, 2023**

Originally published in Italian as Giorgio Agamben,
*La follia di Hölderlin: Cronaca di una vita abitante. 1806–1843*

© 2021 Giulio Einaudi editore s.p.a., Torino

First published in English translation by Seagull Books, 2023
English translation © Alta L. Price, 2023

ISBN   978 1 80309 1 150

**British Library Cataloguing-in-Publication Data**
A catalogue record for this book is available from the British Library

Typeset at Seagull Books, Calcutta, India
Printed and bound by WordsWorth India, New Delhi, India

In his fortieth year, Hölderlin found it
advisable—tactful, even—to lose his mind.

ROBERT WALSER

His house is divine madness.

FRIEDRICH HÖLDERLIN
*from his translation of Sophocles'* Ajax

When one's life of dwelling goes off into the distance . . .
[*Wenn in die Ferne geht der Menschen wohnend Leben* . . .]

FRIEDRICH HÖLDERLIN
'*The View*'

Should,
should a man,
should a man come into the world, today, with
the shining beard of the
patriarchs: he could,
if he spoke of this
time, he
could
only babble and babble
over, over
againagain.
('Pallaksh. Pallaksh.')

PAUL CELAN
'*Tübingen, January*' (*Michael Hamburger trans.*)

**2.** Anonymous, *View of Tübingen*

# CONTENTS

*List of Illustrations*      *ix*

*Translator's Note*      *xi*

Note to the Reader      3

Threshold      5

Prologue      15

Chronicle, 1806–1843      77

Epilogue      295

Catalogue of Books at Hölderlin's House
in Nürtingen      331

Bibliography      339

*Index of Names*      344

# LIST OF ILLUSTRATIONS

1. Portrait of Hölderlin, age sixteen, coloured pencil, 1786. Stuttgart, Württembergische Landesbibliothek, Hölderlin Archive.

2. Anonymous, *View of Tübingen*, watercolour and tempera, mid-eighteenth century. Marbach am Neckar, Schiller-Nationalmuseum.

3. Pass issued by the Bordeaux police, 1802. Stuttgart, Württembergische Landesbibliothek.

4. The tower on the Neckar in a photograph by Paul Sinner, 1868. (Photo © Alamy / Ipa Agency).

5. A copy of *Hyperion* inscribed to Susette Gontard, 1799. Marbach am Neckar, Schiller-Nationalmuseum.

6. Frontispiece of *Die Trauerspiele des Sophocles*, Frankfurt, 1804.

7. Favorin Lerebours, *Portrait of Isaac von Sinclair*, oil on canvas, 1808. Bad Homburg v. d. Höhe, Museum Gotisches Haus. (Photograph © The History Collection / Alamy / Ipa Agency).

8. Anonymous, silhouette of Hölderlin, 1795. (Photograph © Akg Images / Mondadori Portfolio).

9. Napoleon's decree inducting Goethe into the Legion of Honour, 12 October 1808.

10. Wilhelm Waiblinger, *Self-Portrait*, drawing, 1825. Marbach am Neckar, Schiller-Nationalmuseum. (Photograph © Akg images / Mondadori Portfolio).

11. J. G. Schreiner and R. Lohbauer, *Portrait of Hölderlin*, drawing, 1823. Marbach am Neckar, Schiller-Nationalmuseum. (Photograph © Akg Images / Mondadori Portfolio).

12. Cover of the poetry collection published in 1826.

13. Hölderlin family coat of arms (with a branch of elder, *Holder* in German).

14. Detail of a poem signed 'Scardanelli' (1841?). Marbach am Neckar, Schiller-Nationalmuseum.

15. L. Keller, *Portrait of Hölderlin*, drawing, 1842. Marbach am Neckar, Schiller-Nationalmuseum.

16. Detail of a text signed 'Scardanelli' in C. T. Schwab's copy of the poetry collection published in 1826.

17. *Portrait of Hölderlin*, etching after an original charcoal drawing by J. G. Schreiner (1826), circa 1890. (Photograph © Akg Images / Mondadori Portfolio).

# TRANSLATOR'S NOTE

Many translators have brought Agamben's work into English, and long-time readers will recognize in them recurring motifs such as the threshold. All his books engage in a dialogue with philosophers from antiquity to the present. In the original, most of the extended quotes from other languages appear in Agamben's own Italian translation; where I was able to locate published English versions of the same passages, they are credited. Where interpretations differed, I added notes. The author's inclusion of foreign terms in square brackets or parentheses has been maintained.

Hölderlin's late poems appear in the original German and my English for two reasons: not all the selected poems have been published in English; of those that have, all significantly differed from Agamben's Italian interpretations. Honouring both Hölderlin's German and Agamben's Italian called for new English versions. Michael Hamburger's life work on Hölderlin, from Anvil Press Poetry, is recommended reading.

In grappling with what it means to exist, think and interact in certain ways, philosophy has always called upon specialized terminology, which becomes doubly complex in translation. Word choices (*custom/habit, chronicle/chronology, 'Oriental'/Eastern, mode of being/form of life, national/own/native/proper, man/person/human being*, and so on) are always rife with the risk of misunderstanding. I have deferred to Agamben's preference for the universal masculine in his own analyses while also respecting the fact that the German *Mensch* is not exactly the same as *Mann*.

Spelling was less uniform in Hölderlin's day: his and other names (Gok/Gock, Carl/Karl, etc.) appear here as they did in the source documents, and the reader is trusted to understand whom Holterling, Helderle, and other variations refer to.

A *wohnend Leben* or *vita abitante* could also be understood as a 'living life', since *to live* can also be rendered as 'to dwell', 'to reside' or 'to inhabit'. My working title for this book was *Hölderlin, Holed Up* because so much of the world was under stay-at-home orders as it was written and translated, and the last half of the poet's life was the perfect phenomenon to dwell in and dwell on. Circumstances caused many to question what truly living means. May the following pages provide a glimmer from afar.

*Alta L. Price*

*Hölderlin's Madness*

# NOTE TO THE READER

This chronicle of Hölderlin's life was drawn primarily from documentation in the following collections:

Friedrich Hölderlin, *Sämtliche Werke: Grosse Stuttgarter Ausgabe*, VOL. 7, 'Briefe-Dokumente', NOS. 1–3 (Friedrich Beissner and Adolf Beck eds) (Stuttgart: Cotta-Kohlhammer, 1968–1974).

Friedrich Hölderlin, *Sämtliche Werke: Kritische Textausgabe*, VOL. 9, 'Dichtungen nach 1806. Mündliches' (D. E. Sattler ed.) (Darmstadt and Neuwied: Luchterhand, 1984).

Adolf Beck and Paul Raabe (eds), *Hölderlin. Eine Chronik in Text und Bild* (Frankfurt am Main: Insel, 1970).

Gregor Wittkopp (ed.), *Hölderlin der Pflegsohn, Texte und Dokumente 1806–1843* (Stuttgart: J. B. Metzler, 1993).

The historical chronology which has been juxtaposed to Hölderlin's life for the first four years dealt with herein (1806–1809) is drawn primarily, in what concerns Goethe's life, from *Goethes Leben von Tag zu Tag. Eine dokumentarische Chronik,* VOLS 1–8 (Siegfried Seifert ed.) (Zurich: Artemis Verlag, 1982–96). I chose not to extend this historical chronology beyond 1809, because it seemed to me that the juxtaposition with Hölderlin's dwelling life had been sufficiently modelled. Readers can easily continue it on their own by leafing through the aforementioned resource, *Goethe's Life from Day to Day*, or any historical atlas.

# THRESHOLD

In his essay 'The Storyteller', Walter Benjamin describes the difference between a historian, who writes history, and a chronicler, who recounts it, thus:

> The historian is constrained to explain one way or another the events he is describing; under no circumstances can he content himself with presenting them as samples of what occurs in the world. Yet this is precisely what the chronicler does and none more strikingly than his classical representatives, the chroniclers of the Middle Ages, precursors of the modern historians. By basing their accounts of historical events on the inscrutable design of divine providence, they threw off from the start the burden of providing a verifiable explanation. Instead, they offer explication [*Auslegung*], which does not aim to accurately link together specific events, but to embed them in the inscrutable course of the world.[1]

---

1 Walter Benjamin, *The Storyteller Essays* (Samuel Titan ed. and introd.; Tess Lewis trans.) (New York: New York Review Books, 2019), p. 60.

For the chronicler, whether world events are determined by providence or are instead purely natural makes no difference.

Reading the many books handed down to us in the form of 'chronicles' from the late Medieval period onwards—some of which have an undoubtedly historical tone, to begin with—confirms Benjamin's considerations and would seem to suggest the two types can be combined, albeit with a few caveats. First, a chronicle may contain an explanation of the events it retells but, as a rule, the two (record and narration) are clearly separated. Although, for instance, an undeniably historical text such as Matteo Villani's mid-fourteenth-century *Cronica* offers a closely connected narration and explanation, the record of the exact same events as recorded by an anonymous, contemporary chronicler writing in Roman dialect expressly separates the two, and it is precisely this separation that gives his narrative the lively, unmistakeable tone of the classic chronicler:

> During the Lenten period of the year of our Lord 1253, 'twas a Saturday in February, a voice suddenly rose up from the crowd of market-goers in the Roman forum: 'Hear ye, hear ye!' Whereupon the local populace grew livid and began running to and fro like demons. They threw stones at the senatorial palace, and began

looting, especially keen on taking the senator's horses. When Count Bertoldo Orsini heard the commotion, he could think of nothing but saving his own hide and home. Donning all the arms and armour he had, he placed a shining helmet atop his head and spurs at his heels like a real baron. He proceeded downstairs to mount his horse. The screaming and furore reached the unfortunate senator. More sticks and stones rained down on him from above than leaves fall from trees in autumn. Some people really hurled stones, some merely threatened. The senator was stunned by the assault, even cowering under his shield was of no use. Rage had swept through mob across the way as well, near Santa Maria. Over there, due to the heavy barrage of stones, he lost all virtue and conscience. Whereupon the merciless and lawless populace did the deed, stoning him like a dog, hurling rocks at his head as if he were Saint Stephen. Right then and there, the count was cast out of this life. He uttered not a word. Once he was dead, he was just left there, and the people all went home.[2]

---

2 Gustav Seibt, *Anonimo romano. Scrivere storia alle soglie del Rinascimento* (Rome:Viella, 2000), p. 13.

At this point the narrative cuts off and, inserting an incongruous sentence in Latin, the chronicler introduces a cold, logical explanation: 'The cause of such severity was that these two senators had lived like tyrants—they kept exporting grain even as their people starved'. But then this explanation is so non-committal that the chronicler immediately adds another, according to which the violence of the populace was a punishment for how 'Churchly things' had been desecrated.[3] In the eyes of a historian, every event carries a mark, a signature of sorts linking it to a broader historical current, and the event can only make sense seen within that current. The chronicler, on the other hand, adduces reasons whose sole aim is to allow him to catch his breath before launching back into his narration, which has no broader purpose.

The second caveat regards the precise chronological 'concatenation' of events. The chronicler doesn't exactly ignore it, but also doesn't rest content with inserting it into the context of natural history. Thus, in the example Benjamin[4] excerpts from *The Treasure Chest of the Rhenish Family Friend* by Johann Peter Hebel, the marvellous story of the 'grey and wizened' woman who

3 Seibt, *Anonimo romano.*

4 Benjamin, *Storyteller Essays.*

has an 'unexpected reunion' with the fully intact, ice-preserved corpse of her fiancé who died fifty years prior is inserted into a temporal series that juxtaposes historic events from both the natural as well as the human realm: the Lisbon earthquake, the death of Empress Maria Theresa, the farmers' sowing and reaping, the Napoleonic Wars, the English bombardment of Copenhagen, and the millers' milling are all placed on the same level. Similarly, medieval chronicles mark the passage of time with both dates (Anno Domini) and the rhythm of days and seasons: 'as day broke . . .', 'while the sun set . . .', 'it was harvest time, the grapes were ripe, and the people crushed them . . .'. In such chronicles, events to which we usually grant historic importance are assigned no special rank—indeed, they carry the same weight as events we generally ascribe to the insignificant realm of private life and everyday existence. What is different, however, are the timeframe and tempo in which such events take place—this tempo isn't constructed the way 'historical time' is, using chronography to extract such events once and for all from 'natural time'. Rather, it's the self-same time used to measure a river's current or the succession of seasons.

That doesn't mean the events the chronicler recounts are natural. Quite the contrary, they seem to call into question the very notion that history and nature are opposites. Between political history and natural history, the chronicler inserts a third kind of history, one that seems to exist neither in heaven nor in the terrestrial realm but looks at both from up close. Indeed, the chronicler doesn't distinguish between human actions (*res gestae*) and their retelling (*historia rerum gestarum*), almost as if the latter (the narrator's gesture of retelling) were part and parcel of the former (the actions themselves). This is why it never even occurs to the listener or reader to wonder whether the chronicle is true or false. The chronicler doesn't invent a thing, nor needs to verify the authenticity of their sources, whereas the historian simply must verify each and every source. The chronicler's only document is the spoken word—their own voice, as well as the voices from which they've happened to hear the adventure, be it happy or sad, that they then retell.

In our case, use of the chronicle as a literary form has additional significance. As the title of the poem 'Hälfte des Lebens' (Mid-life) prophetically seems to suggest, Hölderlin's life was split neatly in two: his first 36 years, from 1770 to 1806; and the 36 years from 1807 to 1843, which he spent as a madman holed up in the home of Ernst Zimmer, a carpenter. The poet, despite his fears of being removed from communal life, lived the first half of his existence out and about in the

broader world, relatively engaged with current events—
only to then spend the second half entirely cut off from
the outside world. Despite occasional visitors, it was as
if a wall separated him from any relationship to external
events. One emblematic anecdote is that when a visitor
asked him whether he was happy about what was happening in Greece, his only response—in keeping with
what had become a habitual pattern—was: 'This, Your
Majesties, is a question I must not, I cannot answer'.
For reasons that will hopefully become clear to the
reader, Hölderlin chose to expunge all historical
character from the actions and gestures of his daily life.
According to his earliest biographer, he often stubbornly repeated, '*Es geschieht mir nichts*', 'nothing
happens to me'. Such a life can only be the subject of
a chronicle—not of a historical inquiry, much less a
clinical or psychological analysis. In this respect, the
ongoing publication of new documents from the latter
half of his life (in 1991, an important cache was discovered in the Nürtingen archives) has something
incongruous about it and doesn't seem to add anything
new to the already established facts.

This corroborates the methodological principle that a
life's tenor of truth cannot be exclusively defined or
exhausted through words—rather, to a certain extent,
it must remain hidden. A life's tenor of truth is the

vanishing point where multiple events and episodes converge, which are the sole materials that can be discursively shaped into a biography. Although an existence's tenor of truth remains elusive and resists all narrative impulse, it becomes manifest as a 'figure', that is to say, as something that alludes to a meaning that is real but remains hidden. Consequently, only when we reach the point where we perceive a given life as a figure do this life's constituent episodes fall into place and appear in their contingent verisimilitude—meaning they give up any pretence of being capable of providing access to the truth of that life. The moment they reveal themselves as a methodological 'non-path', *a-methodos*, they nevertheless indicate the direction in which the researcher must look. Thus the truth of an existence proves itself irreducible to the vicissitudes and things through which it presents itself to our sight. And yet our eyes, without gazing away from all that, must also contemplate what in that existence only appears as a figure. Hölderlin's life in the tower is the implacable verification of truth's figural character. Although it seems to unfold as a series of more or less insignificant events and habits that Hölderlin's visitors insist upon describing in great detail, nothing can really happen to him: '*Es geschieht mir nichts.*' In the figure, life is purely comprehensible, but precisely because of that, as such, it can never become the object of knowledge. Exposing a life as a figure—as this chronicle aims to—means giving up on knowing it so as to preserve its defenceless, yet untasted knowability.[5]

I have therefore chosen to juxtapose the *chronicle* of Hölderlin's years of madness with the chronology of the *history* of Europe during those same years (including its cultural aspects, which Hölderlin would have been entirely excluded from—at least up until 1826, when the collection of poems edited by Ludwig Uhland and Gustav Schwab was published). It is up to the reader to decide whether, and to what extent in this case—but perhaps more generally as well—a chronicle is truer than a history. In any case, its truth will ultimately depend on the tension which, by estranging it from historical chronology, makes it enduringly impossible to file that chronicle away in the archives.[6]

---

5 In his canto 'Le Ricordanze' (The Recollections), Giacomo Leopardi refers to *la vita indelibata*, the 'untasted life': '*indelibata, intera / Il garzoncel, come inesperto amante, / La sua vita ingannevole vagheggia, / E celeste beltà fingendo ammira*' ('The young boy, / like an untried lover, fantasizes / his illusionary life intact, untasted, / and wonders, dreaming of celestial beauty'). Giacomo Leopardi, *Canti* (Jonathan Galassi ed. and trans.) (New York: Farrar, Straus and Giroux, 2012).

6 *Archiviazione* is a juridical term for the dismissal of a case.

**Bureau**
Des Passe-Ports

3ᵉ 1. N. 1802.

Registre N.

SIGNALEMENT.

Age de *trente ans le*
( *allemand* )
Taille d'un mètre 75 cent
Cheveux
Sourcils
Visage

Front
Yeux
Nez
Bouche
Menton

Signature du Porteur.

Hoffstetter.

N. B.

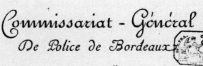

*Commissariat - Général*
De Police de Bordeaux

Bordeaux, le *vingt* du mois de *floréal*
an *dix* de la république Française, une et indivisible.

Le Commissaire-Général de Police
de Bordeaux, invite les autorités civiles et
militaires de la république, à laisser passer et
librement circuler de Bordeaux à Strasbourg
département du bas Rhin le citoyen
professeur d'instituteur
natif de Nürnberg (allemagne) département
demeurant rue N. 1.
et à lui procurer aide et assistance dans
toutes les occasions. d'après les formalités
requises.

Délivré sur le certificat du commissaire de la 4ème

Fait au Commissariat - Général de Police de
Bordeaux, lesdits jour et an.

Les Chef du Bureau,          Le Commissaire-Général de Police,
                             Le Secrétaire Général

**3.** Pass issued by the Bordeaux police, 1802.

# PROLOGUE

Towards mid–May 1802, Hölderlin requests a passport and sets off on foot for Germany. For reasons that remain unknown, he had recently left his post as tutor with the family of Consul Meyer in Bordeaux—a post he had occupied for a mere three months. His journey passes through Angoulême, Paris, and Strasbourg, where on 7 June the police issue him an additional pass. Sometime between the end of June and early July a man appears in Stuttgart, 'emaciated, pale as a cadaver, wild eyes sunk into his skull, his hair and beard grown long, dressed like a beggar', and shows up at the home of Friedrich Matthisson, where, 'in a cavernous voice', he utters just one word: 'Hölderlin'. Shortly thereafter he reaches his mother's home in Nürtingen, in a state that a biography written roughly forty years later describes as follows: 'His facial expression appeared disturbed, he gestured furiously, his condition was one of most desperate madness (*verzweifeltsten Irrsinn*), and his clothing appeared to confirm his claim to have been robbed during his travels.'

**4.** The tower on the Neckar, as seen in a photograph from 1868.

Sixty years later, in 1861, the writer Moritz Hartmann published a story in *Freya*, an 'illustrated magazine for families', titled 'Hypothesis' (*Vermutung*), claiming to have heard the story from a woman identified solely as Madame de S . . . y, who told it to him in her château in Blois.

Approximately fifty years prior, shortly after the turn of the century, when she was fourteen or fifteen years old, she clearly recalled having been out on her balcony and spotting . . .

> a man who, it seemed, was just wandering aimlessly through the fields, as if he were neither in search of anything, nor pursuing any goal. He frequently returned to the same spot without realizing it. That self-same day, towards noon, our paths crossed, but he was so lost in thought that he passed right by without even seeing me. A few minutes later, when we came to a turn and he stopped right before me, he stared off into the distance, his gaze full of an unspeakable nostalgia. These encounters left the rather simplistic girl I was back then absolutely terrified: I ran home and hid behind my father. And yet the sight of that stranger nevertheless filled me with a kind of compassion I couldn't

explain. It wasn't the kind of compassion one feels for a poor man in need of help—even if he certainly looked like one, with his dirty clothes in complete disarray, torn here and there. What filled that little girl's heart with sympathy was a certain noble, somewhat pained expression, as well as the fact that it seemed his mind was utterly absent, lost in the far distance, back with the people he loved. That evening I told my father about this stranger, and he told me he must be one of the many prisoners of war or political exiles out on parole and allowed to live in France's interior.

Days later, the story goes on to say, the girl sees him wandering in the park, along a wide reservoir lined by a balustrade embellished with twenty-some statues of Greek deities: 'When the stranger saw these godlike statues, he quickly strode towards them, filled with enthusiasm. He raised his arms high, in a gesture of adoration, and from up on the balcony it looked to us as if he were uttering words to match his vivid gestures.'

Another time, the stranger spoke to her father, who had let him go for a stroll in the park next to the statues. Smiling, he exclaimed, 'The gods do not belong to human beings—they belong to the world, and when they smile at us, it is we who belong to them.'The father inquires whether he is Greek:'No!—the stranger sighed—Quite the contrary, I am German!' 'Quite the contrary?—my father replied—A German is the opposite of a Greek?' 'Indeed—the stranger brusquely answered, and then a few moments later added—We all are! You, the French, and even your enemies, the English, we all are!'

The description given a few lines later captures the air of nobility and madness the look of the stranger—as the *Madame* calls him throughout her story—exuded:

> He was not handsome, and looked prematurely aged even though he couldn't have been more than thirty; his gaze was spirited yet gentle, his mouth lively and sweet, and it was clear that his threadbare clothing didn't befit his class and upbringing. I was happy my father had invited him into our home. He unceremoniously accepted the invitation and followed us, continuing to talk; every now and then he laid his hand on my head, which simultaneously scared and pleased me. Evidently my father was interested in this stranger, and wanted to listen to his curious conversation at length, but as soon as we reached the salon he was disappointed. The stranger headed straight for the sofa, said, 'I'm tired', and, whispering a

few incomprehensible words, he laid down and immediately fell asleep. We looked at one another, shocked. 'Is he crazy?' my aunt asked, exasperated, whereupon my father shook his head and replied, 'He's an original, a German.'

Over the following days, the overall impression of madness steadily increases:

'All our good thoughts,' the stranger says, speaking about immortality, 'become a Genius, who never abandons us, who always accompanies us, invisible, but with the most beautiful figure, for our entire lives . . . These geniuses are birth, or, if you will, a part of our soul, and that is the only immortal part of it. In their works, the great artists have left us images of their Geniuses, but not the Geniuses themselves'. The aunt asks if that means that he, too, is in some sense immortal. 'I—', he curtly replies, 'you want to know whether I am? I, seated here before you? No! I cannot even think of good. The I that I was ten years ago, though, he is immortal, certainly!' When the father then asks his name, the stranger replies, 'I shall tell you tomorrow. Please believe me, sometimes I have a hard time remembering my own name.'

She sees him one last time, after his behaviour had grown increasingly disturbing, slowly strolling through the park, almost getting lost in the woods.

A workman told us he had seen him sitting on a bench. When he hadn't reappeared after several hours, my father went to look for him. He wasn't in the park. My father scoured the entire district on horseback. He had vanished, and we never saw him again.

A this point the author shares his hypothesis with the narrator: 'This is mere conjecture ... but I believe that you met an extraordinary, noble German poet by the name of Friedrich Hölderlin.'

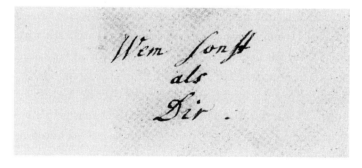

**5.** A copy of *Hyperion* inscribed to Susette Gontard, 1799 (*Wem sonst als Dir,* 'To whom, if not you?').

Although Norbert von Hellingrath includes this 'hypothesis' in his essay on Hölderlin's madness, it would appear to be Hartmann's invention—an embellishment conjured up just as the legend of the mad poet reached its peak—to grab readers' attention.

The clinical diagnosis that C. T. Schwab prematurely signed off on, then, is little more than a projection made in hindsight, purportedly confirming the poet's dementia—a condition that by 1846, the year his biography was published, no one doubted. In truth, the long journey on foot from Bordeaux to Stuttgart had taken its toll: he had been robbed of everything, and his fatigued, malnourished state more than explained his altered appearance. In fact, Hölderlin swiftly recovers and returns to his friends in Stuttgart, only to hear from Sinclair a few days later that his beloved Susette Gontard has died, and the news casts him into deep grief. But he recovers from that blow as well, and in late September 1802 accepts Sinclair's invitation to Regensburg. Later on, Sinclair stated that he had never found Hölderlin more intellectually and spiritually alive than during that visit. Through Sinclair, who acted as diplomat for the imperial estate, Hölderlin meets Frederick V, Landgrave of Hesse-Homburg. He begins work on his translations of Sophocles, and in the following months writes the ode titled 'Patmos', which he then dedicates to the Landgrave on 13 January 1803. He then spends some more time in Nürtingen, and in November writes a letter to his friend Casimir Ulrich Böhlendorff stating that 'the more I study the natural world of my hometown, the stronger its hold on me'. He goes on to say that thenceforth, poets and their work will have to assume a new character, such that, beginning again with the ancient Greeks, poets shall 'sing nationally [*vaterländisch*] and naturally again, with actual originality'.

This carries an implicit reference to a previous letter Hölderlin had written to Böhlendorff dated 4 December 1801, shortly before he set out for Bordeaux, in which he wrote:

> Nothing is harder for us to learn than the free use of what we are born with.[7] And it is my belief that clarity of exposition is originally as natural to us as heavenly fire is to the Greeks ...

---

7 Note that Jeremy Adler and Charlie Louth first translate Hölderlin's *Nationelle* as 'what we are born with', followed by 'national' (which does not have the same exclusively political meaning that the adjective will gradually take on over subsequent decades), and finally 'what is proper to us' and 'what is our own'. The author's Italian renders this concept as *nazionale* and *proprio*, which are in keeping with Adler and Louth's renderings. [Trans.]

It sounds paradoxical. But I put it to you again, for you to verify and make use of as you wish: in the process of civilization what we are actually born with, the national, will always become less and less of an advantage. For that reason the Greeks are not such masters of sacred pathos, because it was native to them; on the other hand they are exceptional in their faculty for exposition . . . With us it is the other way round. That is also why it is so dangerous to derive our aesthetic rules from the sole source of Greek excellence. I have laboured at this for a long time and know now that apart from what must be the supreme thing with the Greeks and with us, that is, living craft and proportion, we cannot properly have anything in common with them. But what is our own has to be learnt just as much as what is foreign. For this reason, the Greeks are indispensable to us. Only it is precisely in what is proper to us, in the national, that we shall never match them because as I said, the free use of what is our own is hardest of all. And it seems to me that your good genius has prompted you to give the dramatic form a more epic treatment. Taken as a whole, it is a genuine modern tragedy. For that is the tragic with us, to go away from the kingdom of the living in total silence packed up in some kind of container, not to pay for the flames we have been unable to control by being consumed in fire.[8]

We should not forget this 'national' turn and the abandonment of the Greek-tragic model that these pages herald if we want to understand both Hölderlin's later thinking as well as his so-called madness.

After months of intense work writing the ode 'Remembrance' (*'Andenken'*) and finishing his translation of Sophocles (a letter written by his friend Christian Landauer informs us that the poet spends 'all day and half the night' writing, to the point that 'it seems his friends no longer exist'), in early June 1803 Hölderlin arrives at the convent of Murrhardt on foot, after 'criss-crossing fields as if guided by instinct'. Schelling and his wife Caroline are at the convent to visit Schelling's parents (his father was a prelate). Just days later Schelling, who had known Hölderlin since their days studying theology at the Tübinger Stift, writes a letter to Hegel that is considered one of the most certain eyewitness accounts attesting to the fact that the poet had already descended into madness:

---

8 Friedrich Hölderlin, *Essays and Letters* (Jeremy Adler and Charlie Louth eds and trans) (London: Penguin Classics, 2009), pp. 334–36.

The saddest sight I have encountered during my stay here was that of Hölderlin. Since his journey to France, whither he had gone at the recommendation of Professor Ströhlin with quite false expectations concerning what would be expected of him, and whence he immediately returned after demands seem to have been made on him that he in part could not fulfil and in part could not reconcile with his sensitive nature—since that unfortunate journey, his spirit has been utterly shattered [*zerrüttet*—this verb will be used repeatedly to designate the poet's condition], and though he is to a certain extent indeed capable of doing some work, e.g. translations from the Greek, his mind is otherwise utterly absent [*in einer volkommenen Geistesabwesenheit*—the term 'absence' will also be used often to characterize his madness]. Indeed, the sight of him unsettled me; he has neglected his external appearance to the point of disgust, and though his speech is less suggestive of madness, he has otherwise wholly assumed [*angenommen*] the mannerisms [*die äusseren Manieren*] of someone in such a condition. There is no hope of curing him here. I thought I would ask whether you might see to him were he perhaps to come to Jena, which he wanted to do.

Pierre Bertaux—a scholar of German, French Resistance leader, and author of several perceptive studies of Hölderlin and his work—has already observed elsewhere that Schelling's account is an outlier, and not without contradictions: Hölderlin is in an 'absent' state, yet still capable of translating ancient Greek (as if translating Sophocles didn't require significant intellectual capabilities); additionally, since his friend's speech remains entirely normal, Schelling can only confirm that he has 'assumed the mannerisms' of a madman—therefore, he is not mad.

The same contradictions appear again in a letter Schelling wrote to Gustav Schwab more than forty years later, four years after Hölderlin's death, recalling his friend's visit to Murrhardt:

> It was a sad reunion, for I soon saw that this delicately strung instrument had been destroyed forever. Whenever I broached a topic that once interested him, his initial response was always correct and appropriate, but by the next sentence he had already lost the thread. I did, however, experience in his company how great is the power of inborn, inherent grace. During the thirty-six hours he spent with us, he said

nothing inappropriate, nor did or said anything contradictory with his earlier noble, proper, courteous nature. It was a painful farewell on the main road—I believe at Sulzbach; I never saw him again after that.

Once again, no information is given to help us comprehend why such a carefully tuned instrument was destroyed. Evidently something in Hölderlin's words and appearance eluded his friend, even though the two had shared such a deep love for philosophy that historians sometimes hesitate to ascribe to one over the other some unattributed texts that have come down to us. The only possible explanation is that, by then, Hölderlin's thinking had grown so far from his own that Schelling preferred to reject it outright.

Even the letters Hölderlin's mother writes to Sinclair reveal the same ambiguity, as if madness had to be proven at all costs, even when the facts seem to disprove it. Sinclair must have realized that her attitude had the potential to harm her son because, following a visit when he did not observe any real 'mental disturbance' (*Geistesverwirrung*), he wrote to her on 17 June 1803 that it must be painful for her son to hear others judge him mad. 'He is too sensitive to not know how to read what lies at the bottom of others' hearts—including their innermost judgments of him.' Since the

Frankfurt publisher Wilmans had agreed to publish the translations of Sophocles that Hölderlin had been hard at work on for months, Sinclair asked his mother to let him come to Homburg, where he would find a friend 'who knows him and his destiny, and from whom he has nothing to hide'. Hölderlin's mother replies that her son, whom she constantly refers to as 'the poor dear' (*der l[iebe] unglückliche*) is unable to undertake such a journey alone, and adds that, 'given his sad state of mind', he would only be a burden to his friends. And yet his condition, as she readily admits, 'has neither improved . . . nor worsened'. What actually strikes his mother as a sign of his insanity is that he is incessantly at work: 'I hoped that if the poor dear no longer had to work as hard as he had over the last year—when not even our prayers managed to distract him from his zealous devotion—his interior state would improve.' 'Unfortunately, his condition has not improved', she wrote in a later letter, 'even if', she reluctantly admits, 'some change has occurred, since the compulsivity he so often suffered has, thank God, nearly vanished.' In May 1804, when Sinclair convinces the Landgrave to offer Hölderlin a position as librarian—a post he readily accepts—his mother objects that 'he is presently unable to accept this position, which, in my humble opinion, requires a certain degree of mental order and clarity. Unfortunately, my dear son's current ability to reason is very weak ...The sheer joy of your illustrious presence and the esteem you show him probably inspired the poor dear to muster up all his mental strength, hence you were unable to notice how completely worn out his mind is.' Her apprehensions only seem to abate two years later, when she manages to have her son admitted to Johann Heinrich Ferdinand Autenrieth's clinic in Stuttgart and, subsequently, arrange for him to be taken in by a carpenter named Ernst Zimmer, where she never once visits him. It is hardly surprising that, at this point, according to records left by Zimmer himself, Hölderlin 'cannot stand his relatives' (*Hölderlin kann aber seine Verwandten nicht ausstehen*).

It is not a matter of ascertaining whether Hölderlin was or was not crazy, nor whether he believed himself to be. What is of decisive importance is that, in fact, he wanted to be so—or, rather, that at a certain point madness struck him as a necessity, something he could not avoid, lest he become a coward, since, 'like old Tantalus . . . the gods had given him more than he could bear'. It has been said of both Swift and Gogol that they did everything they could to go mad, and in the end they succeeded. Hölderlin did not seek madness, he had to accept it; but, as Bertaux notes, his conception of madness had nothing to do with our notions of mental illness. It was, rather, something that could or should be inhabited. That is why, when he translates Sophocles' Ajax, he renders the phrase *theiai maniai xynaulos*, literally 'dwelling with divine madness', as *sein Haus ist göttliche Wahnsinn*, 'his house is divine madness'.

In April 1804, Wilmans publishes Hölderlin's translations of Sophocles' *Oedipus* and *Antigone*, accompanied by two long essays encapsulating the outermost results of Hölderlin's philosophy. It is the last book published in his lifetime and, despite the many typos he bitterly complained of, it is absolutely essential for understanding what he meant when he spoke of the free use of 'what is proper to us' and of the antithesis between the national (*väterlandisch*) and the foreign through which he was rethinking his relationship with the Greek model. In a September 1803 letter to Wilmans, Hölderlin outlines the meaning of his project: 'Greek art is foreign to us because of the national convenience and bias it has always relied on, and I hope to present it to the public in a more lively manner than usual by bringing out further the oriental element [*das Orientalische*] it has denied and correcting its artistic bias wherever it occurs.'

It is particularly significant that Hölderlin chose to exemplify this issue through translations that, many years later, Walter Benjamin deemed 'prototypes of their kind', considering them 'subject to the enormous danger inherent in all translations: the gates of a language thus expanded and modified may slam shut and enclose the translator in silence'.[9] Contemporaries' reception of these translations is equally significant, as exemplified by a letter Heinrich Voss wrote in October 1804: 'What do you think of Hölderlin's Sophocles? Is our friend really a raving madman or is that just an act, such that his Sophocles stealthily satires bad translators? A few nights ago, I was with Schiller and Goethe, both of whom were amused by this translation. Just read the fourth chorus of Antigone—you should have seen how Schiller laughed!' Schelling's verdict, in a letter he wrote to Goethe in July that same year, is equally harsh: '[Hölderlin] is in a better state than last year, but still visibly in a state of disarray [*Zerrüttung*]. His translation of Sophocles reflects his deteriorated state of mind.' Although it may be difficult to overlook such superficial judgments, not to mention Schiller and Goethe's obtuse laughter, they nevertheless remain the most explicit proof of the immeasurable gap between what Hölderlin had in mind and the culture of his time. His goal—translation as both calque and correction of

---

9 Walter Benjamin, 'Die Aufgabe des Übersetzers', in *Gesammelte Schriften* IV, 1 (Frankfurt am Main: Suhrkamp, 1972); 'The Task of the Translator' (Harry Zohn trans.), in Rainer Schulte and John Biguenet (eds), *Theories of Translation* (Chicago: University of Chicago Press, 1992), p. 82.

# DIE TRAUERSPIELE

DES

# SOPHOKLES.

ÜBERSETZT

VON

FRIEDRICH HÖLDERLIN.

*ERSTER BAND.*

FRANKFURT AM MAIN, 1804

BEI FRIEDRICH WILMANS.

**6.** Frontispiece of *Die Trauerspiele des Sophocles*, 1804.

the original—was so unheard of that his contemporaries could only view it as a demented idea. (In 1797, when Goethe read the poems 'Der Aether' and 'Der Wanderer', he had not laughed, instead deeming them 'not altogether improper' (*nicht ganz ungünstig*) and advising the young Hölderlin to 'write short poems and devote himself to subjects of some interest on the human level'.)

Hölderlin's translations from both Sophocles and Pindar were done during the same period, and neither attempt to find semantic equivalents of the foreign language in the poet's own—a notion that was and largely remains a widely held concept of what translation is. Rather, his versions appear to aim, as has been aptly observed, at achieving a sort of 'mimesis', if not downright 'mimicry', of the original's form.[10] Following an approach even Cicero considered misguided, Hölderlin not only translates *verbum pro verbo,* 'word for word', but forces the syntax of his German to adhere to the Greek. His pursuit of a 'literal' translation is so obsessive that he freely coins neologisms structured to correspond to the original (the Greek *siderocharmes,* which dictionaries

---

10 Michael Theunissen, *Pindar. Menschenlos und Wende der Zeit* (Munich: C.H. Beck, 2000), p. 959; see also Felix Christen, *Eine andere Sprache* (Schupfart: Engeler, 2007), p. 23.

typically translate as 'bellicose', is etymologically rendered *eisenerfreuten*, 'iron-happy'). The result of such extreme 'hyperliterality'[11] is that the translation often seems to stray so far from the meaning of the original that less prudent critics have claimed he committed outright translation errors, attributing them to his 'relatively limited knowledge of Greek' or 'lack of adequate reference material'.[12] It is no surprise, then, that even as generous a reader as Schwab could write that such an 'entirely literal' translation was incomprehensible without the original.

Norbert von Hellingrath's 1910 dissertation on Hölderlin's *Pindarübertragungen* marked the beginning of a gradual shift in critical opinion. Drawing a distinction in Greek rhetoric between two ways of harmonizing individual words within the semantic context of the sentence, Hellingrath refers to a 'flat construction' (*glatte Fügung*), in which individual words are rigidly subordinated to the syntactic context, and a 'rigid construction' (*harte Fügung*) of the sort Hölderlin used, whereby each word tends to isolate itself to the point

---

11 Wolfgang Schadewaldt, 'Hölderlins Übersetzung des Sophokles', in *Über Hölderlin* (Frankfurt am Main: Insel, 1970), p. 244.

12 Schadewaldt, 'Hölderlins Übersetzung des Sophokles', p. 243.

of nearly full independence from its surroundings, so that the overall meaning is often open to multiple interpretations and the reader has the impression of being faced with 'an unusual and foreign language'.[13] Benjamin builds upon Hellingrath's suggestion in his essay 'The Task of the Translator' to distinguish between translations that aim solely to reproduce meaning and those in which meaning is 'touched by language only the way an aeolian harp is touched by the wind',[14] because the translator aims—just as Benjamin maintains Hölderlin did—at precisely that which cannot be communicated by language. Ever since, countless studies have followed in Benjamin's footsteps, reversing traditional prejudices to deem Hölderlin's translations a veritable 'poetological paradigm'. Such analyses privilege 'foreignizing' translations over 'domesticating' ones in which the translator attempts to remain invisible.[15] Hölderlin's purported translation errors are now viewed as 'creative errors' (*schöpferische Irrtümer*)[16]

13 Norbert von Hellingrath, 'Hölderlins Wahnsinn', in *Zwei Vorträge. Hölderlin und die Deutschen; Hölderlins Wahnsinn* (Munich: Bruckmann, 1922), p. 23.

14 Benjamin, 'The Task of the Translator', p. 82.

15 Lawrence Venuti, *The Translator's Invisibility: A History of Translation* (London and New York: Routledge, 1995), p. 5.

16 Schadewaldt, 'Hölderlins Übersetzung des Sophokles', p. 247.

or as the result of 'artistic wilfulness' (*künstlerische Gestaltungswille*).[17]

Yet one cannot understand the essence of Hölderlin's translations and their mimesis of the original's form without first defining the goal they sought to attain. As has been observed,[18] Hölderlin in no way intended to enrich German-language literature with new translations; rather, he wanted to address a problem that was both personal as well as historical and philosophical. His aim was nothing less than to push the ancient Greek approach to composing poetry to its extreme, through his German (or 'Hesperian', as he would call it in his notes on Sophocles) versions, in order to expose its core nature and, at the same time, 'correct' its errors.

Consider what is clearly set out in his letter to Böhlendorff: the theorem according to which the 'free use' of 'what is proper to us' is the most difficult thing implies that the Greeks, for whom heavenly fire and passion is the proper, national element (and thus also their weak point), will achieve excellence through

---

17 Jochen Schmidt (ed.), *Friedrich Hölderlin: Sämtliche Werke und Briefe*, VOL. 2 (Frankfurt am Main: Deutscher Klassiker, 1990), p. 1328.

18 Wolfgang Binder, *Hölderlin und Sophokles* (Tübingen: Hölderlinturm, 1992), p. 21.

what is foreign to them, namely clarity (which Hölderlin also terms a 'Junoesque sobriety'). The Hesperians, to whom sobriety and clarity belong, will instead excel in celestial fire and passion, which are foreign to them, while they will be weak and clumsy when it comes to clarity. Hence the complexity of the double operation that takes place in translating from the Greek: on the one hand, we have the Greeks, who have repudiated their own 'national' element in order to excel in the gift of exposition and, by emphasizing the 'Oriental' element, are restored to their 'national element', celestial fire, which is also their weakness; on the other, in an inverse symmetry, we have the Hesperians, who excel in the kinds of passion and heavenly fire supposedly foreign to them and, by comparison with the Greek model whose 'straying ways' they correct, are restored to the clarity of exposition which is, however, also their weakness.

It is only in relation to this arduous and twofold task that the obsessive adherence to literalness and the obscurity that characterize Hölderlin's translations acquire their true meaning: the Junoesque sobriety that the Greek poet achieved is rendered opaque and almost illegible to the same degree that the Hesperian translator sees his own clarity bending to the foreign demands of passion and its correction, while at the same time signalling us towards the weak and missing 'national' element. The free use of the proper is, then, a bipolar operation in which the national and the foreign—what is offered up as a kind of dowry and the otherness that stands before it—are rendered closer through their divergent agreement. And the only poet up to the task is one who, by translating, risks losing his own language in this polar tension. Translation is not, therefore, just one more literary operation among so many others: rather, it is the privileged poetic place par excellence, in which the free use of the proper is borne out. And that—both for the poet and for all peoples— is the most difficult task.

It becomes evident that such a task cannot be tackled by a poet whose ability to reason, according to contemporary criteria, remains intact. As Benjamin intuited, in an operation so tensely carried out in the realm between language's two opposing polarities, 'meaning plunges from abyss to abyss, until it threatens to become lost in the bottomless depths of language'.[19] Dementia and madness, however, are not at issue here. Rather, the issue is a dedication to one's task—a dedication so intense that one doesn't hesitate to sacrifice formal, artistic excellence for the sake of a poetic manner that is ruinous, unhinged, and, taken to the extreme, incomprehensible. After his translations from

---

19 Benjamin, 'The Task of the Translator', p. 82.

Sophocles, Hölderlin carries out this paradoxical task in two ways: initially, he chooses the highest poetic form of the Greek tradition, the hymn, and, as the *Homburger Folioheft* eloquently shows, breaks it up and methodically deconstructs its articulation through extreme parataxis and 'rigid construction'; subsequently—in the quatrains written while holed up in his tower—he instead chooses the humblest and most naïve poetic form of his native tradition and monotonously, repetitively adheres to its simple, rhymed structure.

Philosophy is born when certain individuals realize that they can no longer feel part of a people, that a people like the one poets believed they were addressing does not exist, or that it has become something foreign or hostile. Philosophy is, above all, this exile of a human being among other human beings, the predicament of being a stranger in the city in which the philosopher lives and in which he nevertheless continues to dwell, obstinately addressing an absent people. Socrates epitomized this paradox of the philosophical condition: he became such a stranger to his people that they sentenced him to death; but then, by accepting his sentence, he joins the people once again—as the one whom they have irrevocably expelled.

From a certain moment onwards, at the threshold of modernity, even poets become aware they can no longer address their own people—even the poet understands he is speaking to a people that no longer exists or, if it does, it cannot and does not want to listen to him. Hölderlin himself is the point at which these contradictions explode, and the poet is forced to recognize himself as a philosopher or—as he put it in a letter to Christian Ludwig Neuffer—take refuge in the hospital of philosophy. He realizes that what he lacks, or rather his weak point, is a sense of community with his people—what he referred to as the 'national'— without which he will never be able to excel poetically. Hence the rupture, the break with earlier poetic forms, the paratactic shattering of the hymn, the stereotypical repetitions of his final quatrains; hence Hölderlin's unconditional acceptance of the diagnosis—madness— his people ascribed to him. And, nevertheless, he continues writing until the very end, stubbornly seeking out a 'German song' in the darkness of night.

The theorem regarding a free use of the proper is not the result of abstruse thought; upon closer inspection, it relates to concrete problems whose relevance is now particularly visible. It deals with two categories that are useful for understanding the historical development not only of every individual, but also of every culture. As Gianni Carchia intuited, Hölderlin transforms the poetic problem of tragedy into a problem of the philosophy of history.[20] He terms the West's two fundamental tendencies *national* and *foreign*: the former drives the West to find itself in the proper; the latter estranges it, pushing it out of itself. It goes without saying that in reality the national and the foreign, which Hölderlin exemplifies by comparing Germany and Greece, both belong to every individual and every culture (in Hölderlin's words, to every nationality). It is all too evident that what has happened is that the West owes its immense modern-day success to the fact that it is willing to almost unconditionally abandon its native element (its religious and spiritual traditions) in order to excel in a realm that can be defined as foreign (the economic and technological sphere), in which, however—according to the Hölderlinian paradigm— it was destined to excel from the very start. In such a situation, it is only natural that reactive movements spring up and try to reclaim the native element in some way—that is, by trying to 'translate' the foreign into the more familiar terms of the national tradition; it is equally inevitable, however, that these attempts become entangled in difficulties and contradictions that these movements—or their poets, according to Hölderlin—cannot come to grips with. The free use

---

20 Gianni Carchia, *Orfismo e tragedia*, NEW EDN (Macerata: Quodlibet, 2019), p. 72.

of the proper is truly the most difficult thing. In any case, in both his life and his poetry, Hölderlin tried to experience the contrast between these two fundamental tendencies and their potential reconciliation, whatever it might cost him.

The fact that Hölderlin's mental condition during this period did not compromise his lucidity is proven not only by his intense poetic and philosophical productivity but also by his lively interest in political affairs. Indeed, it is precisely because of his political involvement that the problem of his madness first exploded beyond the private sphere, taking the form of an official medical diagnosis on 5 April 1805.

Since the root of Hölderlin's political involvement lay in his friendship with Isaac von Sinclair, it is worth pausing to discuss this rather memorable man who had a decisive influence on the poet's life. Sinclair was born in Homburg in 1775 (five years Hölderlin's junior), and because of his family background was predestined for a political career under the landgrave of the small state of Hesse-Homburg. His father had been the landgrave's tutor, and the young Sinclair was therefore educated alongside the princes. In March 1795, after two years studying law at the University of Tübingen, Sinclair met Hölderlin at the University of Jena, where he had

**7.** Favorin Lerebours, Portrait of Isaac von Sinclair, 1808.

enrolled to study philosophy, and had also attended Fichte's lectures during the winter semester of 1794–95. In a letter dated March 1795, he announces to a friend that he has made the acquaintance of 'magister Hölderlin', a 'close friend *instar omnium*':

> He is young and at the same time affable; his immense culture makes me ashamed, pushing me towards admiration through imitation; I plan to spend next summer with this radiant, amiable, exemplary man on a solitary garden estate. From my solitude and from this friend I expect worthy results. I am considering finding a position for him as tutor to the princes, as I would like to have him near going forward, at all costs.[21]

During their years in Jena, the two friends developed a shared philosophy, as is evident in the *Philosophische Raisonnements*, finally published in 1971, which should be read alongside *Urteil und Sein* (Judgement and Being), a piece Hölderlin wrote in early 1795 on endpapers torn from a book—Beissner posits it could well have been Fichte's 'Doctrine of Scientific Knowledge', which Hölderlin's text powerfully calls into question.

---

21 Hannelore Hegel, *Isaac von Sinclair. Zwischen Fichte, Hölderlin und Hegel* (Frankfurt am Main: Klostermann, 1971), p. 30.

GIORGIO AGAMBEN

Indeed, Hölderlin's fragment opens with a radical critique of Fichte's 'absolute I' in which both subject and object are identified in self-consciousness. Therefore, what Fichte posits at the outset is in fact nothing more than the 'original division' (*die ursprüngliche Trennung*) through which subject and object, 'intimately united in intellectual intuition', separate and, as such, become possible. But precisely insofar as they consist only in an *Ur-teilung*, in an 'original split', in which object and subject are in mutual relation, they imply 'the necessary presupposition of a whole, of which object and subject are the parts'. The Fichtean 'I am I' is 'the most fitting example of this theoretical split' that Hölderlin intends to question. But the concept of being he contrasts to the Fichtean 'I' implies a union of subject and object, in which no split is possible. 'Where subject and object are united absolutely and not merely partially, so that no split can be posed without injuring the unity of what is to be separated, there and nowhere else can one speak of an absolute being (*Sein schlechthin*), as occurs in intellectual intuition.'[22]

This absolute being must not be mistaken for the identity of the Fichtean I: 'When I say: I am I, the

22 Friedrich Hölderlin, 'Der Tod des Empedokles. Aufsätze', in *Sämtliche Werke*, Kleine Stuttgarter Ausgabe, VOL. 4 (F. Beissner ed.) (Stuttgart: Kohlhammer, 1962), p. 226.

46

subject I and the object I are not united in such a way that no separation can be posed, without harming the essence of what is to be separated. On the contrary, the I is only possible through this separation of the I from the I.' At this point Hölderlin names the other object of his critique: self-consciousness (*Selbstbewusstsein*). 'How can I say, "I!" without self-consciousness? I set myself in opposition to myself, I separate me from myself, but despite this separation I recognize me as the same me in its opposite.' Since the identity that underlies Fichte's doctrine does not imply any real unity of object and subject, 'then', the fragment peremptorily concludes, 'identity is not = to absolute being'.[23]

Sinclair's *Philosophische Raisonnements* agree so completely with Hölderlin's line of thinking that one can imagine them reflecting and discussing their ideas together. Here, the separation Hölderlin identified in the Fichtean position of the I is defined as reflection. 'What takes place, what is there in reflection? A separation takes place, unity is posited as something that ought to be . . . separating actually means reflecting and positing. The I is not a substance, it exists only in

---

23 Hölderlin, 'Der Tod des Empedokles', p. 227.

reflection.'[24] Sinclair's critique of Fichte—and, essentially, all idealism—is explicit: 'In such a doctrine of science, I can only give the acts of my spirit as they are presented in reflection' (p. 268). In fact, reflection coincides with the very form of all knowledge and all science, hence a critique of reflection implies a critique of knowledge:

> The task of knowledge [*Wissen*] goes beyond the form of knowledge. The limit of knowledge is the limit of the consciousness of an I; knowing is possible only for an I. The form of all knowing is reflection. What is outside of reflection I can only experience through the negation of my knowledge, insofar as I show that the fault lies in my knowledge—that I cannot know, and I create distance from forms of knowledge. To unite God (the *principium activum*), the I, and matter (the *principium passivum*) in such a way as to suppose something beyond an ideal is an indispensable task. (p. 271)

To the indissoluble being of Hölderlin's fragment there corresponds what Sinclair calls 'peace' (*Friede*) or *athesis*, non-position: 'Originally it was peace, *athesis*.

---

24 Hegel, *Isaac von Sinclair*, p. 267. [The following three quotations are from the same source.]

There was reflection and there arose the harmonious confusion of one-sided points of view that had not yet been separated in the practical sphere.'

If reflection seeks to understand this non-position, it decays into an I:

> As soon as one wants to know *theos* (the 'athetic' unity, the essence), one transforms it into an I (Fichte's absolute I). Inasmuch as one reflects on its supreme essence and posits it, one separates it, and after separation one again gives it its character of non-separation by means of a unification, whereby in some way the being of separation is presupposed: the imperfect concept. (pp. 268–69)

Using a notion likely derived from Hölderlin— whose essay 'Mode of Procedure of the Poetic Spirit'[25] speaks of a 'transcendental sensation' (*transzendental Empfindung*)[26]—Sinclair deploys a play on words, calling *aeisthesis*, 'eternal sensation', the principle by which the opposition between thesis and athesis, position and non-position, is overcome.

---

25 *Verfahrungsweise des poetischen Geistes*, presumably written in the autumn of 1799; the title, missing from the manuscript, is Zinkernagel's.

26 Hölderlin, 'Der Tod des Empedokles', p. 270.

Even from this brief overview it is clear that what Hölderlin and Sinclair were pondering was nothing less than another possible way—an alternative to the path Fichte's idealism had paved. It is therefore no surprise that Schelling and Hegel had to keep their distance from the spiritual route their companion from Tübingen was embarking upon. In his later writings, Hölderlin entrusts not knowledge, but poetry with the task of capturing the athetic being that necessarily evades reflection. As he unreservedly affirms in his essay on the poetic spirit, the poetic 'I' can live up to its task and grasp that 'infinitely united and living unity' that reflection can grasp only as nothingness and, even then, only on condition of being able to grasp itself.

> The hyperbole of all hyperboles, the boldest and most supreme attempt of the poetic spirit—if ever it succeeds in attaining it—is to capture the original poetic unity, the poetic I, the poetic self; by such an attempt, it would at once both abolish and preserve [aufhöbe] its individuality and its pure object, the united and the living, the harmonious and mutually active life.[27]

---

27 Hölderlin, 'Der Tod des Empedokles', p. 263.

This hyperbole of all hyperboles is precisely what Hölderlin seeks to bring to fruition in the years between 1800 and 1805.

In this regard, a textual detail in the letter to Böhlendorff deserves special attention. Speaking to his friend about how his drama approached the Western element, Hölderlin writes: 'It [the drama *Fernando*] is, in its totality, a *genuine* modern tragedy' (*eine ächte moderne Tragödie*). It is noteworthy that Hölderlin calls this drama a 'modern tragedy' even though the work's subtitle (*Eine dramatische Idylle*) announces that it is technically an idyll—that is, an essentially antitragic poetic genre. Hegel, in his *Lectures on Aesthetics*, defines the idyll as a poetic genre that 'abstracts every deeper universal interest of spiritual and ethical life to depict humankind in its innocence'.[28] This is the opposite of a tragedy, which Hegel claims is centred on an unresolvable conflict between guilt and innocence. Hegel discusses the idyll at length: a key feature is that 'nature seems to easily satisfy every need that arises in man', as in the golden age; as for the authors of idylls, he says 'Gessner is the most boring, hence no one reads him any more.'[29] And yet the idyll must still have occupied

---

28 G. W. F. Hegel, *Aesthetics: Lectures on Fine Art* (T. M. Knox trans.) (Oxford: Clarendon Press, 1975), p. 1221.

an important place among literary genres, if Goethe could refer to *Hermann und Dorothea* as a *bürgerliche Idylle* and call it, with evident self-satisfaction, *mein idyllisch-episches Gedicht*. Similarly, in his *Athenäums-Fragmente*, Schlegel defines the idyll as 'the absolute confluence of ideal and real'.[30] But it is Schiller's essay 'On Naïve and Sentimental Poetry' (*Über naive und sentimentalische Dichtung*), where an entire section is devoted to the idyll, that most fully confirms the special rank of this literary genre. Schiller defines the idyll as a poetic form in which 'all opposition between the real and the ideal is abolished' and all conflict 'both in the individual man and in society' is completely resolved. Insofar as the idyll 'represents man in the state of innocence, in a condition of harmony and peace with himself and with everything outside himself',[31] Schiller likens it to comedy, in which 'man looks around himself and into himself, always with peace and clarity'. Thus, in a letter to Humboldt dated 30 November 1795, he writes that if a perfect idyll turns

---

29 Hegel, *Aesthetics*, p. 1222.

30 Friedrich Schlegel, *Kritische Ausgabe,* VOL. 2: *Charakteristiken und Kritiken* (Munich, Paderborn and Vienna: Schöningh, 1967), p. 204.

31 Friedrich Schiller, 'Über naive und sentimentale Dichtung', in *Sämtliche Werke,* VOL. 5 (Munich: Hanser, 1962), pp. 750, 744.

PROLOGUE

out to be impossible, then 'comedy would be the highest poetic work'.[32]

Why, then, does Hölderlin call an idyll—a form that is not only antitragic, but borders on comedy—a modern tragedy?

The extreme evolution of Hölderlin's thought coincides with his reflections on the three successive drafts of the tragedy *The Death of Empedocles*, to which he devoted his energies between spring 1798 and early 1800. As has been observed elsewhere, the tormented process that repeatedly leads Hölderlin to abandon the draft in progress and undertake a new, substantially different one corresponds to his progressive deconstruction of the very notion of tragedy, which ultimately results in the reduction of his tragic text to an 'unfinished torso'.[33] A significant example is the long fragment I shall refer to as 'Empedocles' Reason', in which the act of reconciliation that tragedy should perform through the death of the individual is ultimately revealed to be inadequate and illusory. Here, the tragic is defined by the contrast between the organic, meaning the limited and conscious individuality of art, and the

32 Stephan Kraft, *Zum Ende der Komödie. Eine Theoriengeschichte des Happyends* (Göttingen: Wallstein, 2012), p. 173.

33 Mariagrazia Portera, *Poesia vivente. Una lettura di Hölderlin* (Palermo: Aesthetica Preprint, Supplementa, 2010), p. 100.

aorgic, or unlimited and incomprehensible nature. As
the tragedy unfolds, each of these two elements passes
into its opposite, and what was split is restored to its
original unity. But this moment—the climax of tragic
sentiment—also coincides with the death of the individual: 'It centres on the struggle and death of the
individual: the moment in which the organic sheds its
ego, its particular existence, which had become an
extreme, and the aorgic sheds its universality—not as
it would in an ideal fusion, but rather in an extreme
and very real struggle.'[34]

The result of this struggle in which two extremes
transgress into their opposite is, therefore, their reconciliation: 'extreme enmity actually seems to be extreme
conciliation' (p. 160). Significantly, however, this reconciliation is immediately declared merely apparent
(*scheinbar*), even deceptive. Since reconciliation was
only a product of conflict, each of the two elements
again tends towards the extreme, 'so that the unifying
moment dissolves like a hallucination [*Trugbild*] . . . and
the happy deception [*der glückliche Betrug*] of reconciliation ends' (p. 160). If Empedocles is, then, a sacrificial
victim (*Opfer*) of his time, the reconciliation his death

---

34 Hölderlin, 'Der Tod des Empedokles', p. 159. [The following three quotations are from the same source.]

achieves is illusory, and this illusoriness invests the tragic form itself:

> Thus Empedocles had to become a victim of his time. The problems of fate among which he had grown up had to be apparently [*schein-bar*] resolved in him, and this resolution had to prove apparent and temporary, as in more or less all tragic characters, all of whom are more or less attempts—in their characters and manifestations—to resolve the problems of fate, and all of whom negate themselves insofar as they are not universally valid . . . in the same way, the one who appears completely to resolve problems of fate is also the most conspicuous victim—above all in his transience [*Vergänglich-keit*] and in the escalation of his repeated attempts. (pp. 163–64)

Hölderlin abandons his last draft of Empedocles because he realizes that the death of the sacrificial victim can only offer the appearance of reconciliation, and that a 'modern tragedy' is only possible on condition of renouncing the very idea of a sacrificial death. Thus the disconcerting statements in his letter to Böhlendorff—which would otherwise seem almost comic—become clearer: 'For that is the tragic with us, to go away from the kingdom of the living in total silence packed up in some kind of container, not to pay for the flames we have been unable to control by being consumed in fire.'

In any case, the disappearance of the sacrificial victim from modern tragedy—or, rather, anti-tragedy—is of decisive significance. In a particularly dense paragraph of his note on Antigone, Hölderlin outlines two modalities of the tragic word's status: the Greek and the Hesperian. If every tragic representation consists of a word that acts (*in dem faktischen Worte*), the word of Greek tragedy acts in a mediated way (*mittelbarer faktisch wird*) in that it grasps a sensible body and 'the body it grasps it actually kills' (*wirklich tötet*).[35] The Hesperian word, on the other hand, does not need physically to kill because it acts without mediation and 'grasps a more spiritual body'. A later passage clarifies the meaning of this contrast, distinguishing between two characteristics of the word, which Hölderlin expresses with two adjectives that are not immediately obvious but whose meaning leaves no doubt:

And so, the deadly-factual [*das tödlichfaktische*], the real murder through words [*der wirkliche Mord aus Worten*] is to be considered more as

---

35 Friedrich Hölderlin, 'Ubersetzungen', in *Sämtliche Werke*, VOL. 5, Kleine Stuttgarter Ausgabe (F. Beissner ed.) (Stuttgart: Kohlhammer, 1954), p. 293. [The following four quotations are from the same source.]

essentially Greek, which form of art is subordinated to a more national form of art. A
national one, as may well be demonstrated,
may be more a killing-factual [*tötendfaktisches*],
than a deadly-factual word [*tödlichfaktisches*];
it would not actually end with murder or
death, because this is where the tragic must be
grasped, but end more in the manner of the
*Oedipus at Colonus*, so that the word from an
inspired mouth is terrible, and kills, but not in
a Greek, palpable way, with an athletic and
sculptural spirit, where the word overwhelms
the body, so that the latter kills. (p. 294)

Here, the sacrificial victim that defined Greek
tragedy disappears, because the word addresses a 'more
spiritual body' (p. 293)—that is, it acts immediately as
a word, through itself and on itself, without the mediation of a physical death. The 'more spiritual body' that
it grasps is the word itself, which, as Hölderlin goes on
to explain a few lines later, 'must be intellectually
understood and vitally appropriated' (p. 295).

An earlier passage of the same note on Antigone
addresses how the very impossibility of tragedy assumes
an aspect of 'sublime mockery', which coincides
with madness: 'sublime mockery [*der erhabene Spott*]—
insofar as sacred madness [*heiliger Wahsinn*] is the highest human manifestation, and here it is more soul than

language—surpasses all other expressions' (p. 291). It is significant that, at this point in the tragedy, during the transition from Greek to Hesperian (*wie es vom griechischen zum hesperischen gehet*), madness is presented as the highest human manifestation and, at the same time, is defined as sublime mockery—as if tragedy here ventures beyond itself to take an antitragic turn that, in some regards, might call to mind comedy.

Hölderlin repeatedly reflects on poetic genre, particularly in two fragments on the difference between poetic genres ('Über den Unterschied der Dichtungsarten') and on variations of tone ('Wechsel der Töne'). He always mentions the epic, the lyric, and the tragic, trying to not only define the characteristics of each but also how they interrelate. It is worth recalling that, as Emil Staiger suggested,[36] poetic genres belong not only to the realm of literature, they also name several 'fundamental possibilities of human existence'. Strikingly, these texts make no mention of the comic genre. Yet in a letter to Clemens Brentano dated 20 September 1806, Sinclair does include a few reflections on the idyll and the comic, which were likely also touched upon in his ongoing, impassioned discussions with Hölderlin. In this letter, Sinclair contrasts the

---

36 Emil Staiger, *Grundbegriffe der Poetik* (Zurich: Atlantis Verlag, 1946), p. 226.

idyll—a comedic form par excellence—with tragedy and Romantic poetry. 'It seems to me,' he writes about one of Brentano's poems,

> that it is a genuine idyll, that is, a naïvely comic [*naiv comisch*] poem, unlike a Romantic poem, in which the soul appears more deeply moved and the poet—albeit not out of cowardice—proceeds to expound upon it . . . Perhaps you aren't interested in my thoughts about genre regarding your poem. But philosophy is perennially on my mind, and therefore I believe one should always be familiar with the purest examples and general principles of the idyll . . . The idyll always strikes me as indirectly comic—that is, it belongs to the highest and noblest comic genre. The Romantic, on the other hand, seems only tragic, and even in our most ancient German novels, which abandon tragedy entirely, a balance is never struck between the tragic and the comic.[37]

Hölderlin must also have been familiar with the pages in which Schiller, after contrasting tragedy and comedy, assigns comedy the higher rank, writing that

---

37 Michael Franz, '1806', in *Le pauvre Holterling, Blätter zur Frankfurter Ausgabe* (Frankfurt: Rote Stern, 1983), p. 46.

'if comedy achieves its purpose, it renders all tragedy superfluous and impossible [*sie würde . . . alle Tragödie überflüssig und unmöglich machen*].'[38]

Hölderlin's apparent silence regarding comedy is still more difficult to explain. It is as if, despite having understood that tragedy had become impossible, he simply could not see any way beyond tragedy except through madness—but then madness had to assume the character and manner of a comedy, of 'sublime mockery'. Hence the exaggerated courtesy with which he simultaneously welcomes visitors and keeps them at a distance, deploying titles like 'Your Majesty', 'Your Holiness', 'Your Highness' and 'Mister Baron, Sir—*oui monsieur . . .* '; hence the nonsensical words he enjoys surprising them with: '*Pallaksh, pallaksh*', '*Wari wari*'; hence the sublime irony with which he tells those who ask him for a poem, 'Shall I write about Greece, about spring, or about the spirit of the age?'; or the way he abruptly points out to a visitor, 'You see gracious sir, a comma!' while reading a page from his own *Hyperion*.[39] Seen from this perspective, the late, monotonous,

---

38 Schiller, 'Über naive und sentimentale Dichtung', p. 725.

39 Wilhelm Waiblinger, *Friedrich Hölderlins Leben, Dichtung und Wahnsinn* (Leipzig: Brockhaus, 1831); reissued in D. E. Sattler (ed.), *Friedrich Hölderlin: Sämtliche Werke, Kritische Textausgabe*, VOL. 9 (Darmstadt: Luchterhand, 1984), p. 156.

rhyming quatrains he signed as Scardanelli are, according to Sinclair's criteria at least, idylls; they certainly belong to the 'highest and noblest comic genre'.

After Hölderlin's time in Jena and the two years (1796–98) as a tutor in the Gontard household in Frankfurt, when Homburg served as a refuge of sorts, his friendship with Sinclair in Homburg is happily prolonged. 'Your lord son', Sinclair writes to Hölderlin's mother on 6 August 1804,

> is perfectly well and at peace. I, as well as six or eight others who have spent time with him here, are convinced that what appears to be a mental disturbance [*Gemüths Verwirrung*] is not that at all—rather, it seems to be a mode of expression he has assumed for well-hidden reasons [*aus wohl überdachten Grunden angenommene Äusserungs Art*]—so we are all glad to enjoy his company . . . He is living in the home of a French watchmaker named Calame, in the very neighbourhood where he wanted to live.

Precisely as in Schelling's account, Hölderlin's apparently extravagant behaviours are referred to as 'assumed' mannerisms, not madness. All contemporary accounts highlight the contrast between Hölderlin's outward appearance and mannerisms and his verbal expressions. One of Sinclair's friends, Johann Isaak

Gerning, notes in his diary entry for 28 June 1804:
'Sinclair came over with Hölderlin, who has become a
librarian, but is also a poor melancholic devil: *quantum
mutatus ab illo*' (how changed from what he once was).
In a later note he writes, 'This morning Sinclair and
Hölderlin lunched at my place. The latter praised my
"Saeculare" [a poetic composition about the eighteenth
century] and said that Ramler, on the other hand,
hewed to an overly strict, antiquatedly lyrical tone . . .
I rejoice indeed to have found a true poet here.' In any
case, Hölderlin's mother remains resolute, replying to
Sinclair that the letter she received from her son after
a long silence, far from reassuring her, instead made her
fear that his sad state had worsened.

At this point, political events abruptly intervene in
Hölderlin's life, changing everything. Sinclair, whose role
as *Regierungsrath* meant he carried out important diplo-
matic missions on behalf of the landgrave, had gotten
involved with an unscrupulous young opportunist
who went by the name of Alexander Blankenstein and
had proposed a lottery to solve the small state's financial
problems. In June 1804 Sinclair, accompanied by
Blankenstein and perhaps even Hölderlin, had several
meetings with Christian Friedrich Baz, burgomaster
of Ludwigsburg, and their mutual friend Leo von
Seckendorf, both of whom had been influenced by the
libertarian ideas of the French Revolution. We can

only guess at the tenor of these discussions, but what is certain is that, faced with Napoleon's aggression—and victories that were already shaking the tenuous foundations underlying multiple confederations—Sinclair and his friends saw a need for greater democracy, thinking it the only way the Germanic states could hold their own. By the time Sinclair realized Blankenstein was less than reliable and cancelled the lottery, the latter took revenge by publicly denouncing Sinclair. On 29 January 1805 Blankenstein went before the prince-elector and accused Sinclair of preparing an attempt on the life of the prince and his minister, Count Wintzingerode.

On 7 February, in a clarification requested by the minister, Blankenstein describes Sinclair as 'a dangerous atheist' who plans to 'make Swabia the first theatre of anarchic war'. Curiously, he also mentions Hölderlin, albeit with some reservations: 'His comrade Friedrich Hölderlin of Nürtingen, who was likewise privy to the whole thing, has fallen into a kind of madness [*eine Art Wahnsinn*], constantly railing against Sinclair and the Jacobins and shouting, much to the amazement of the locals, "I don't want to be a Jacobin" [*ich will nicht Jacobiner sein*].'

Almost immediately, the situation rapidly declines. Despite a pretence of resistance from the landgrave,

Sinclair is arrested at two o'clock in the morning on 26 February and—in front of nearly one hundred spectators, a crowd that might have included Hölderlin—taken to Schloss Solitude in the Duchy of Württemberg, where he is imprisoned. Blankenstein, in a further statement to the investigating magistrates, states that he had travelled with Sinclair and Hölderlin from Stuttgart to Homburg, and claimed 'Hölderlin knew of Sinclair's plans' but that 'recently Hölderlin has gone nearly insane [*fast wahnsinnig geworden*] and violently swears at Sinclair, shouting, "I don't want to be a Jacobin, *vive le roi!*".'

Since Hölderlin was now in danger of being arrested, the landgrave made a statement on 5 March to the investigating judge in an attempt to clear his name:

Sinclair's friend, Magister Hölderlin of Nürtingen, has been in Homburg since July of last year. For some months now, he has fallen into such deep desolation, that he should be treated as if [*so als*] he were really insane [*Rasender*]. He incessantly cries out, 'I don't want to be a Jacobin, down with all the Jacobins! I shall stand before my kind prince-elector with a clear conscience.' The landgrave wishes that the extradition of this man, should there be an inquiry, be treated with utmost restraint. If, however, it is deemed necessary, the poor soul should be taken into custody and cared for in perpetuity because, in that case, he would not be permitted to return to Homburg.

It is entirely possible that, given the seriously risky situation in which he found himself, Hölderlin decided to exploit the suspicions of madness that hung over him to effectively make an escape. This hypothesis would seem to be confirmed by the tone of his exclamations, which sound calculated to distance himself from the culprits (he insults his friend von Sinclair) and from the revolutionary plot in which he might otherwise have been implicated. Even if Bertaux's supposition that Hölderlin was indeed a Jacobin is misguided (in a letter to his brother Karl in July 1793, Hölderlin joyfully welcomes the news of Marat's death, calling him 'the infamous tyrant' and sympathizing with Brissot, who represented the Girondins), he certainly followed what was happening in France quite closely. He therefore had no reason, other than utilitarian self-preservation, to cry *vive le roi*, nor to sympathize with the prince-elector and Wintzingerode, who were both notoriously anti-democratic. In any case, feigned or not, his demeanour achieved its intended aims. On the other hand, during the interrogation he was immediately subjected to, Sinclair not only confirmed his friend's altered state of mind ('He only rarely experiences *dilucida intervalla*'), but also decisively stated that he had never heard Hölderlin say that he did not want to be a Jacobin, which was certainly also true.

The judge overseeing the trial contacts the deanery and consistory of Nürtingen for additional information about Hölderlin, and they confirm his abnormal state: despite the 'good disposition', the 'good gifts and diligence' of 'magister Hoelderle' [*sic*], his 'excessive studies' and his 'sick imagination' had produced a 'confusion [*Verwirrung*] of his soul'. Finally, upon the commission's request a doctor in Homburg, *Physicus Ordinarius* Georg Friedrich Karl Müller, issues a certificate on 9 April that officially attests—albeit with some reservations and in a style unburdened by scientific rigour—to Hölderlin's state of madness, thereby freeing him from all possible charges:

> I can only partially fulfil the task entrusted to me regarding Magister Hoelderlin, as I am not his doctor, and therefore do not know his condition in depth. All I can say is that the aforementioned Magister Hoelderlin already suffered from a strong hypochondria when he arrived here in the year 1799 . . . No means

could cure it, and he left here with it. Since then, I had no more news of him until last summer, when he returned, and I was told that 'Hoelderlin is back, but he is mad'. Remembering his hypochondria, I found the rumour rather inaccurate, but I wanted to see for myself whether it was real, so I tried to talk to him. How astonished I was when I found the poor man so distraught [*zerrüttet*] that no one could have had a reasonable conversation with him, prey as he was of such violent agitation. I visited him a few more times, but I always found the sick man worse and worse, his speaking grew incomprehensible. Now his madness has escalated into fury [*Raserei*], so that it is absolutely impossible to understand the speeches he gives, which sound part German, part Greek and part Latin.

From this moment on, whatever his mental state, the poet is somehow obliged to honour the diagnosis that saved him from being arrested. In the months that follow, he leaves his room in the watchmaker Calame's home and moves into the home of a saddler named Lattner, where he plays the piano 'night and day'. On 19 June, he meets with Gerning, whose diary entry records—with the same ambiguity it had a year before—the poet's positive judgment of a didactic poem he had drafted: 'Poor Hölderlin even praised my thoughts, but also told me not to make them too moral. When he speaks thusly, is it with a healthy or a sick mind?' A few weeks later, in a letter to Goethe, Gerning himself informs us that Hölderlin continues to work on his translations from Pindar ('Hölderlin, who is still half-crazy, is actively at work on Pindar'). On 9 July, Sinclair is acquitted of all charges and returns to Homburg, where he finds his friend in a peaceful state. In Berlin that September he meets Charlotte von Kalb, who—in a letter to Jean Paul reflecting on her conversations with Sinclair—writes of Hölderlin: 'This man is now furiously mad [*wütend wahnsinnig*]; what is more, his mind has ascended to such a height that only a visionary inspired by God can reach.' He is deemed half mad but perhaps sane, furiously mad and yet visionary: assessments of Hölderlin's condition continue to oscillate between two radically opposite poles.

On 24 September, Princess Maria Anna of Hesse-Homburg writes to her sister, Landgravine Auguste of Hesse-Homburg, that she has been reading Hölderlin's *Hyperion* for months: 'Ah, how I love this book! What has become of its author?'

On 29 October, in the only letter to her son that has come down to us, Hölderlin's mother admits to having given her son reason to hate her: 'Perhaps without knowing it or wanting to, I caused you to feel aversion towards me . . . be good now, stay in touch, I shall try to improve.'

Even the most careful interpreters of Hölderlin's life and work continue to view the poet's extreme spiritual path through the lens of tragedy. Bertaux suggests Hölderlin saw his own life through the Hegelian paradigm of the tragic hero—simultaneously guilty and innocent—and that after the death of Susette Gontard he somehow felt responsible. 'Only a hero,' he writes, 'who is both innocent and guilty—like Oedipus, like Antigone—can be a tragic hero . . . Only through a combination of guilt and innocence does the hero become a tragic figure.'[40] Peculiarly, while noting that Hölderlin almost never uses the word 'guilt' (*Schuld*), Bertaux assumes an analogy with and even dependence on the Hegelian paradigm of the tragic. The exact opposite is true: as Gianni Carchia has observed, Hölderlin represents an attempt to escape from the dialectic of the tragic and its false reconciliation of opposing extremes:

---

40 Pierre Bertaux, *Friedrich Hölderlin* (Frankfurt am Main: Suhrkamp, 2000), p. 600.

Hölderlin contrasts the sacrificial mysticism
and the tragic union in death of the opposite
poles of art and nature with an entirely different possibility for removing conflict. Noting
that it is already present in the work of
Sophocles, the possibility he envisions is finite
and eccentric, rather than infinite and imma-
nent. . . . Compared to the positive solutions
of post-Kantian idealism, which have often
considered the trope of tragic death a key
archetype of dialectical resolution, Hölderlin's
position is instead configured as abiding with
the Kantian tension of the negative.[41]

Right at the end of his 'Remarks on *Oedipus*',
Hölderlin contrasts the tragic-dialectical reconciliation
of conflict between the divine and the human with a
disarticulation and disconnection, which he formulates
as a truly eccentric notion of 'sacred betrayal':

In order to ensure the course of the world has
no gaps and *the memory of the celestials does not
end*, God and man communicate with each
other in *the all-forgetting form of infidelity*, since
divine infidelity is to be kept in mind more than
anything else. Thus, man forgets himself and

---

41 Carchia, *Orfismo e tragedia*, p. 74.

God turns, but in a sacred way, like a traitor. At
the extreme limits of passivity, in fact, there are
no other conditions beyond time and space.[42]

Not only does the sacred turning or 'betrayal' here
take the form of a disarticulation and forgetfulness that
excludes any possibility of dialectical reconciliation, but,
as Hölderlin's note to *Antigone* suggests, the characters
of the tragedy are also removed from their 'ideal figure'
(*Ideengestalt*) and situated in a decidedly antitragic—if
not properly comic—dimension. They are not, in fact,
'engaged in a dispute about truth, not fighting for their
reason; and not like one who fights for life or property
or honour . . . rather . . . they oppose each other as persons in the narrower sense, as persons of rank, and
formalize' (p. 296). The character's shift from tragic to
comic, characterized by his class (*ceto*), is confirmed
by the fact that the tragic conflict is emptied of its content and becomes purely formal, so that it is no longer
a struggle for life and death, but rather—invoking
an image that sounds undeniably comic—'a contest
between runners, where the one who first runs out of
breath and jostles against his opponent has lost' (p. 296).

---

42 Hölderlin, 'Übersetzungen', p. 220; Adler and Louth trans.,
p. 484. [The following two quotations are from the same
source.]

71

Hölderlin conceives of and experiences the absence of the gods, which he considers the condition of his time, in an equally antitragic way. Those who have dwelt on the atheology of late Hölderlin, from Blanchot to Heidegger, never seem to tire of quoting the passage from 'Bread and Wine' in which the poet unreservedly declares that as the gods take their leave—since mere mortals are unable to bear their fullness—'perplexity / and sleep assist us: distress and night-time strengthen'. Equally if not more oft cited is the correction of the last two lines of the poem 'The Poet's Vocation' ('Dichterberuf'), in which Hölderlin states just as peremptorily that the poet 'needs no weapons and no cunning, / as long as God's absence comes to his aid'. And yet commentators do not seem to realize that here, with a sort of theological nihilism which perhaps not even Nietzsche could have managed, the death or absence of God is in no way tragic, nor is it a matter of waiting for another divine figure, as Heidegger suggested in his later work. With a profound and paradoxical intuition—whereby the poet, 'like ancient Tantalus', is allowed to see more than he can bear—Hölderlin situates humans' leave-taking from the gods in the poetic and existential form of an idyll or comedy.

There is a text—one which has remained in the shadows among all Hölderlin's other theoretical

writings—in which he reflects on the meaning of
comedy and, much as Sinclair had, mentions it alongside the idyll. In Hölderlin's review of Siegfried
Schmid's play *The Heroine*, published in 1801, he
develops a veritable theory of comedy whose full
import deserves to be acknowledged. The review
opens with a digression (*Umschweife*)—he even apolo-
gizes for its length—in which he tries to both define
comedy and refute 'the unfair prejudice' against this
genre. True comedy aims to give a 'a true but poetically
grasped and artistically presented copy of so-called
ordinary, habitual life' (*des sogennantes gewöhnlichen . . .
Lebens*). This in turn is immediately defined as that 'life
that stands in a weaker and more distant relation to the
whole and for that very reason will be infinitely significant when it is comprehended poetically, but to a
high degree insignificant in itself'.[43]

What is essential in comedy, then, is that same
'common, ordinary, habitual' (*Gemeine und Gewöhnliche*)
element—the very element that, in his November
1798 letter to Neuffer, Hölderlin had reproached
himself for having avoided. And if what is at issue in
habitual life is a weakening of the relation to the

---

43 Hölderlin, 'Der Tod des Empedokles', p. 300; Adler and
Louth trans., p. 460. [The following three quotations are from
the same source.]

whole, the poet who wants to represent it poetically 'must tear each time a fragment of life from its vital context' and yet at the same time 'resolve and mediate' (*lösen und auszumitteln*) the contrast of what, through this separation, appears 'excessive and one-sided' (p. 301). And he can do this not so much by 'elevating it and making it perceptible' as such, but rather by presenting it as a 'natural truth' (*Naturwahrheit*); 'And precisely where his subject is drawn most from reality, as in the idyll and comedy and elegy, he will above all have to make up for his theft by giving it an aspect of aesthetic truth, by presenting it in its most natural relation to the whole' (p. 301).

What happens in comedy is that what is most common and insignificant—ordinary, habitual life— becomes 'infinitely significant' (*unendlich bedeutend*) and, although isolated from its vital context, shows itself as a truth of nature. *But isn't this precisely what, in the thirty-six years he spent holed up in his tower, Hölderlin's life and poetry stubbornly, exemplarily and comically sought to do?* And isn't 'habitual' life the self-same inhabiting, 'dwelling' life (*wohnend*, that is, living according to habits) that appears so distant and done in the last idyll written from that tower? *Wenn in die Ferne geht der Menschen wohnend Leben* . . . 'When one's life of dwelling goes off into the distance . . . '. In any case, if Hegel defines idylls as 'poems that are half descriptive and half lyrical, having nature and the seasons as their main subject', then the poems from the tower—that extreme, incomparable poetic legacy of the West—are, technically, idylls.

**8.** Anonymous, silhouette of Hölderlin as Magister, 1795.

*Chronology, 1806–1843*

# 1806

*1 January.* France abolishes the revolutionary calendar and returns to the Gregorian calendar.

*In January*—having defeated the Austro-Russian troops commanded by Kutuzov at the battle of Austerlitz in December 1805 and signed the Treaty of Pressburg on 26 December of that year—Napoleon proposes the formation of a confederation of small German states under the protection of France. The Rheinbund is officially established on 12 July 1806, and shortly thereafter leads to the dissolution of the Holy Roman Empire, which immediately has disastrous consequences for Hölderlin.

*14 January.* From Goethe's diary: 'At the theatre this evening, rehearsals of Stella . . . Since, according to our culture's custom of monogamy, the relationship of a man with two women is considered unacceptable—particularly as presented here—this is necessarily a tragedy.'

*31 January.* Goethe—who unofficially serves as cultural attaché for the duchy of Weimar while also suffering from a urinary disorder—exclaims in conversation, 'Ah, if only the good Lord would bestow upon me of one of those healthy Russian kidneys slain at Austerlitz!'

**14 January.** Hölderlin's mother asks the Nürtingen consistory for financial assistance to cover her ailing son's caretaking expenses, which 'have already consumed the inheritance received from his father'. Per consistory records, 'The widow of Pastor Gok requests a stipend for her son, M. Hoelderlin, during his illness. Hold until further notice.'

**April.** Sinclair returns to Homburg from Berlin, where he had published a poem dedicated to Hölderlin.

**30 April.** Per Nürtingen consistory records: 'The widow of Privy Councillor Gok requests a stipend to support her son, the ailing M. Hoelderlin. TBD.'

**11 June.** Per Nürtingen consistory records, 'The widow of Privy Councillor [*CammerRath*] Gok requests support for her son, the ailing M. Hoelderlin. Conclusion: Since neither the exhibit previously submitted nor the enclosed notification makes it possible to ascertain the current whereabouts of M. Hoelderlin, the deanery of Nürtingen should be informed. Subsequent conclusion: Recommend to the Superior Department of Finance the sum of at least 100 thalers in order to proceed.'

**13 February.** *Napoleon writes to the Pope: 'Your Holiness may be sovereign in Rome, but I am Emperor. All my enemies must also be your enemies.' Four days later, the emperor orders the construction of a triumphal arch at the Place de l'Etoile. On 21 March, Pius VII replies to Napoleon: 'Your Majesty affirms in principle that You are Emperor of Rome. We answer with apostolic frankness that the sovereign Pontiff—who after so many centuries has become sovereign of Rome, as no other sovereign can boast— does not now, nor ever has, recognize any other power superior to his own throughout his States.'*

**30 March.** *After French troops quell a Bourbon rebellion in February and King Ferdinand withdraws to Sicily under the protection of the English fleet, Joseph Bonaparte assumes the title of King of the Two Sicilies.*

**30 April.** *From Goethe's diary: 'At noon, experiments and conversations with Riemer. In the evening,* Cosí fan tutte *at the theatre.'*

**24 June.** *Letter from Goethe to Hegel, with a rescript from Minister Voigt guaranteeing Hegel a salary of 100 thalers enclosed: 'My dear Sir, the enclosed document is proof that I have not stopped working for you behind the scenes. Naturally, I'd have liked the sum to be larger—but in cases*

As a result of the formation of the Confederation of the Rhine and dissolution of the Holy Roman Empire, the small state of Homburg is incorporated into the Grand Duchy of Hessen-Darmstadt. Sinclair fears losing his position serving the Landgrave. Understandably worried by this new situation, on 3 August he writes, perhaps prematurely, a letter to Hölderlin's mother asking that she return her son to Nürtingen:

> Most Honoured Madame Councillor,
>
> The changes that have regrettably taken place in the Landgrave's situation, of which you must also have heard, have forced certain restrictions upon him and make my continued presence here inadvisable. It is therefore no longer possible for my unfortunate friend, whose madness has reached a new peak, to continue receiving a salary and remaining here in Homburg, hence I have been asked to request that you send for him. His odd behaviour has irritated the rabble, who are now so against him that in my absence the gravest ill-treatment of his person may be feared, but for him to remain free may be equally dangerous to the public. Since there are no adequate institutions here, he must

*like this one, a good start confirms that much has already been gained for the future.'*

*17 July. The Federation des Souverains du Rhin is created in Paris. Sixteen southern German princes sign the Rhein-bundesakte, thereby placing themselves under the protection of Emperor Napoleon and committing to provide him with troops and money in return. The small state of Homburg, where Hölderlin is lodged, is incorporated into the Grand Duchy of Hessen-Darmstadt.*

*4 August. Goethe leaves the baths at Karlsbad, where he had gone on the advice of his doctor, and sets out for Weimar. 'Left Eger early, around six in the morning. Bad weather . . . Found a fruit seller in Hasch who sold us 6 little pears for 1 little coin. Heavy rain. Around seven in the evening: news of the official declaration of the Confederation of the Rhine under the French protectorate . . . On 1 August the German princes of the confederation formally seceded from the Holy Roman Empire. Reflections and discussions. Dinner was good.'*

*8 August. 'Left at six in the morning. En route we talked politics and came up with new titles for Napoleon: "We, Napoleon", "God Has Our Back", "Muhammad of the World", "Emperor of France", "Imposer and Protector of the Empirical Universe", etc. . . . Also rediscovered one of Fichte's* be removed from public life as a precaution. You can well imagine how much this pains me, but necessity must prevail over sentiment, and these times have already accustomed us to such constraints. It shall be my duty to take care of Hölderlin as well as possible in the future, too, but present circumstances prevent me from saying anything more.

On behalf of my mother and myself, please rest assured—you and your family have our ongoing friendship and total esteem.

Yours most devotedly,
Dr Isaac von Sinclair

It is possible that, in order to convince Hölderlin's mother, Sinclair exaggerated the seriousness of his friend's condition, which just a few months earlier he had described as calm. On the other hand, the 'restrictions' mentioned in the letter did not imply that Sinclair's duties had ceased, since he remained in the Landgrave's employ and was actively working to prevent the dissolution (known as *Mediatisierung* in the bureaucratic terminology of the time) of the state of Homburg. Anticipating more frequent work travel, Sinclair likely thought of entrusting Hölderlin to *doctrines in the acts and proceedings of Napoleon . . . Went back to the tavern of the gold star. Light lunch . . . '.*

*This same day, in his role as informal diplomat, Goethe sends a letter to the police commissioner in Jena:*

> *My servant Gensler, who has been staying with me for some time now and had previously performed his duties to my satisfaction, has recently treated my family and companions in the rudest, harassing, coarse, and choleric manner. Reprimands and threats have produced only temporary results, and I have had to endure great inconvenience . . . During our journey to Karlsbad, his undocile demeanour exceeded all bounds, and he not only treated my fellow passengers shamefully, but during the return journey as well he behaved cruelly and with extreme perfidy towards the coachman . . . I ask that you confiscate all of the aforementioned Gensler's belongings and take him into custody until the matter is resolved, such that I and my companions may be protected from his behaviour, which verges on that of a raging madman.*

**9 August.** *As Napoleon's influence in Germany expands, Frederick William III, the king of Prussia, mobilizes the army, forms an alliance with Russia and England, and declares war on France.*

his mother without being able to imagine the consequences of his letter.

Hölderlin's mother decides to have her son taken to Professor Autenrieth's clinic in Tübingen, without even having him travel through Nürtingen to assess his condition herself. He is admitted on 15 September. The supervised transport costs 137 Gulden.

**11 September.** Caroline of Hesse-Darmstadt, Landgravine consort of Hesse-Homburg, writes to her daughter, Princess Maria Anna of Hesse-Homburg:

> *Le pauvre Holterling a ete transporte ce matin pour etre remis a ses parents il a fait tous Ses efforts pour se jetter hors de la Voiture mais l'homme qui devoit avoir soin de lui le repoussa en Arriere, Holterling crioit que des Arschierer l'amenes et faisoit de nouveaux efforts et grata cet homme, au point, avec ses ongles d'une longueur enorme qu'il etoit tout en sang.*

The poor Holterling (*sic*) was transported this morning, and is to be handed over to his parents. He made every effort to throw himself from the coach, but the man who was tending to him pushed him back. Holterling yelled, struggled, and badly scratched the man; since

*19 August.* *Goethe writes to one Professor Luden: 'This fragment, titled* Faust, *is only one part of a great, sublime— indeed, divine—tragedy. This tragedy, once finished, shall portray the spirit of all world history; it will depict all human life, encompassing past, present, and future . . . Faust represents all humanity.'*

*1 September.* *'Left Jena around eight in the morning. Read Horace's* Ars Poetica *en route to Weimar. Sudden storm. In the evening went to a comedy,* Minna von Barnhelm *by Lessing. The first two acts are fine, good plot and development. The third act stagnates, losing all coherence.'*

*6 September.* *'Drank water from Eger. Continued geognosy project. Went to the library. Spent afternoon at the wedding of Herr von Pappenheim to Fräulein von Waldner.'*

*11 September.* *'Drank water from Eger. Visited his Most Serene Highness [Charles Augustus, Grand Duke of Saxe-Weimar and of Saxe-Eisenach] at the Römische Haus.'*

*16–17 September.* *'Spent the evening with his Most Serene Highness, preparing for some errands in his absence . . . And bidding him farewell upon his departure [to serve as general in the Prussian Army].'*

his fingernails were so long, the man was covered in blood.

According to Werner Kirchner:

> It was the morning of 11 September 1806 when the coach that was to take Hölderlin home arrived. The madman had to be pushed in by force. He repeatedly tried to escape, and each time the man accompanying him pushed him back to his seat. Hölderlin shouted that the guards were taking him away and defended himself with his extraordinarily long fingernails, to the point that his companion was covered in blood. This proves what madness had overcome him. The memory of Sinclair being imprisoned in Württemberg the year before had been seared into his mind.

Both the Landgravine and Kirchner, whose accounts seem to stem from the same source, incorrectly state that Hölderlin was to be taken to his mother's house. The anecdote of Hölderlin's forced transfer was added to the end of the Landgravine's letter, perhaps at a later date. The passage immediately preceding it jokingly refers to another scene of 'madness', which perhaps inspired the inclusion of Hölderlin's: '*La nouvelle Duchesse de Nassau est à Francfort depuis mardi penses M.*

*13 October. In Jena, Hegel witnesses the first French van-
guard enter the city, and shortly thereafter sees Napoleon on
horseback. That same day he writes to his friend Niethammer:
'I saw the emperor—this soul of the world—go out from the
city to survey his reign; it is a truly wonderful sensation to
see such an individual, who, concentrating on one point while
seated on a horse, stretches over the world and dominates it.'*

*14 October. The French army roundly defeats Prussian
troops at Jena and Auerstädt, and the first French infan-
trymen enter Weimar, sacking the city. As Duke of Weimar,
Charles Augustus had allied with Prussia, and although
Goethe was in the duke's service, he and his colleague
Friedrich Wilhelm Riemer welcome the French soldiers at the
city gates, offering them wine and beer, and assuring them
that there are no more Prussian troops in Weimar. In order to
protect his property from plunder, Goethe puts his home at
the disposal of Marshal Ney and his entourage. Despite a
few incidents that night, the plan succeeds, and his house is
spared ('We are alive! Our house was saved as if by a miracle
from the looting and the fires').*

*'On that unhappy night,' he later writes to his publisher
Johann Friedrich Cotta, 'my greatest concern was for my
papers, and rightly so. Thefts in other houses had done serious
damage, with others' papers either destroyed or scattered all
over the place. Going forward, as soon as I get through this*

*de Bismarck le fameux est rentre au service et on dit a cet heure qu'il est devenu fol et que sa folie s'est decline a table qu'il a jette des boules de paines à la figure de ma Cousine.'* ('The newly appointed Duchess of Nassau has been in Frankfurt since Tuesday. The illustrious Mr de Bismarck has returned, but some now say he has gone mad, and his madness grew worse at the dinner table, such that he threw bread in my cousin's face.')

As for Kirchner's account, it is contradictory. On the one hand, he explains Hölderlin's resistance by attributing it to his fear of being arrested like Sinclair—which is certainly understandable, given that he was being forced into the carriage. But then, on the other hand, that same fear is used as proof of his madness. The stubbornness with which Hölderlin tried to escape can be explained perfectly if one assumes, as is more than likely, that his companions had informed him of their journey's true destination.

Records from the *Clinicum für Wahnsinnige* in Tübingen laconically record Hölderlin's stay: 'Magister Hölderlin of Nürtingen, from 15 September 1806 to 3 May 1807, 321 days.'

Michael Franz, in his meticulous reconstruction of the events of September 1806, has pointed out that the journey between Homburg and Tübingen could *period, I will be even more prompt to have my manuscripts published.'*

**15 October.** *Napoleon arrives in Weimar while Charles Augustus is away commanding a Prussian vanguard, and is immediately received by Duchess Louise, who goes on to claim that he treated her 'très impoliment'. One eyewitness account reports that Napoleon told her, 'Je vous plains, Madame. J'écraserai votre mari' ('I pity you, Madam. I am going to crush your husband'). In all likelihood, Goethe, 'powdered up and dressed for court', was present at their meeting. In any case, his diary entry for this same day reads: 'At court for the arrival of the emperor.'*

*Over the following days and months, Goethe—now understandably concerned about his future—makes new arrangements regarding his personal, legal and financial situation. Had Napoleon decided to dissolve the Duchy of Weimar, which was entirely possible, Goethe would have lost his annual income of 1,900 thalers and likely also the house he was living in, which he did not yet officially own. On 19 October, Goethe marries Christiane Vulpius, whom he was already living with, and legally recognizes their son August.*

**19 October.** *'Goethe—with his bride, his son, and myself as witness—went to the castle church. The marriage was celebrated in the sacristy. Conveniently, the senior consistory* hardly have taken four days (11 to 15 September), and suggests instead that Hölderlin, as a letter from Frau von Proek to Zwilling seems to imply, was temporarily lodged in a hut.

Johann Heinrich Ferdinand Autenrieth, director of the clinic in Tübingen, had studied medicine in Pavia and was not a psychiatrist by today's standards. His clinic did, however, tend to the mentally ill, and he had invented a mask to prevent them from screaming. According to his own accounts this muzzle of sorts, when used in combination with a simple hand-tie—which he claimed was more effective than a straitjacket—had the power to calm patients. There is no record of whether Hölderlin was subjected to this treatment.

> I have had a mask made from shoe-sole leather, it covers the chin from underneath, and at the height of the mouth has a protuberance of thin, softly padded leather on the inside. An opening is cut for the nose, and two for the eyes. Two horizontal strings attach the mask to the head, passing above and below the ears, around the nape of the neck. A third, wider string runs vertically around the sides, tightening the base of the mouth opening from below; it can be adjusted by a buckle above the head, so as to prevent the patient from opening their

*advisor, Günther, performed the ceremony' (Friedrich Wilhelm Riemer); 'With respect to his marriage, Goethe said that in times of peace one can ignore the laws, but in times like these one must obey them' (Johanna Schopenhauer); 'I could not be a well-wisher at Goethe's marriage, so preferred to remain silent' (Charlotte von Schiller).*

**20 October.** *Vivant Denon, Napoleon's arts commissioner, asks Goethe to pose for a profile portrait executed by the engraver Benjamin Zix.*

**October 21.** *Goethe writes to Minister Voigt: 'Might Your Excellency send me 100 or 200 thalers, since I have little money left for the winter and must tend to things in Jena? Money flows from my pockets like water through a sieve.'*

*Goethe writes to Vivant Denon:*

> Je me fais des reproches, que pendant Votre présence, mon estimable ami, je ne sentis que la joye de Vous revoir et que j'ai oublié la misère qui m'entoure. A peine êtes-Vous parti, que les maux, dont l'Academie de Jena est accablée, me sont représentés de nouveau par quelques dignes membres ...
>
> *I feel deep self-reproach; during your presence, my esteemed friend, I felt only the joy of seeing you*

mouth while the soft padding presses the lips together. I tie the patient's hands at their back using a soft cotton cord, and let them walk around for a half hour or even an hour . . . I would like to propose this innocent mask as a necessary tool in any institution for the insane. I have always found the straitjacket too tiresome and difficult to put on a madman intent on defending himself. Certainly, simply tying the patient's crossed hands at their back with a cotton string is easier. This treatment need seldom be prolonged, nor must this mask be worn for more than an hour. The result is that the patient experiences relief for many hours or half days, often even a bout of voluntary calm lasting several days or entire weeks.

Clinic records report the following prescriptions for Hölderlin:

16 September, in Autenrieth's handwriting:

| | |
|---|---|
| Belladonna, | 6 grams |
| Digitalis purpurea, | 2 grams |

in an aqueous infusion of chamomile with aniseed
one tablespoon, 3 times a day

*again, and completely forgot the misery that sur-*
*rounds me.The moment you left, the evils burdening*
*the Academy of Jena swiftly returned, in the form of*
*some of its esteemed members . . .*

**24 October.** *Goethe writes to Cotta:*

*Happily, proofs of the fourth volume (of my works)*
*just arrived . . . for this and the others, already*
*received, I am generally satisfied. Above all, let us*
*thank God for having reached this point . . . I am*
*now more eager than ever to publish my manuscripts.*
*The time of hesitation is past—gone are the leisurely*
*hours in which we flattered ourselves with the hope*
*of one day realizing things we had only begun to*
*plan.*

**12 November.** *'Reviewed ten sheets of proofs of the* Theory
of Colours *. . . After lunch, Meyer. Spent the evening at*
*Madame Schopenhauer's with Fernow, Meyer, Councillor*
*Ridel, Schütze.' 'Goethe was in a rare mood—he told one*
*anecdote after another, and was truly splendid. Rarely have*
*we laughed so hard . . . '. 'In response to Fernow's observa-*
*tions, he told us about Italy, the Italian language, and its dif-*
*ferent dialects.'*

17 and 18 September, in Justinus Kerner's handwriting:

same prescription, 4 tablespoons

18 September, in Autenrieth's handwriting:

250 ml wine for two days

21 September, in Kerner's handwriting:

As before

21 September, in Autenrieth's handwriting:

| | |
|---|---|
| Tincture of Cantharidin, | 2 grams |
| Sweet mercury, | 16 grams |
| Pure opium, | 4 grams |
| White sugar, | 1 ounce |

Mix and divide into 8 equal parts

Administer the powder in 4 doses

30 September, in Kerner's handwriting:

Repeat as before

## 9 October. Stuttgart

Ministry Report and Royal Ordinance:

Hölderlin, on account of his early talent, had
excellent prospects. After rigorous study, he
won a scholarship and accepted a post as a

*On **November 16**, Prussia, now defeated, signs a truce with France at Charlottenburg. The following December the peace treaty of Posen is signed, whereby the Duchy of Weimar joins the Rheinbund as a sovereign state. 'This small confirmation of our political existence is of great significance for us,' writes Minister Voigt to Ambassador von Müller. The price is equally significant: the duke commits to placing 800 men at the disposal of the emperor, and to provide quarters for 80,000 French soldiers and 22,000 horses through the spring of 1808. He is also obliged to pay France 2.2 million francs, a sum equivalent to the entire duchy's annual income.*

*Between **25 and 29 December**, Goethe writes a long letter to the duke, asking that his affairs be settled once and for all. 'For the people presently dear to me,' he writes,*

> *and whom I wish to provide for, the sole possession I can rely upon is the house you so generously provided me, although one last step remains to finalize ownership . . . The moment this is completed, I and my loved ones shall have occasion to celebrate. It will be as if a solid foundation has been lain under our feet after so many days when we felt this tenuous arrangement trembling over our heads, threatening to collapse.*

tutor abroad, returning home in 1804. Signs of a nervous illness immediately appeared, with periodic bouts of mental illness due, according to his doctor in Nürtingen, to an excess of night-time study and insufficient physical exercise. Regrettably, given the circumstances, a full recovery is unlikely. Meanwhile, his mother has made every effort to tend to her son's health and now finds herself, having exhausted the resources inherited from his father, forced to appeal to Your Royal Majesty for support.

The Royal Department of Finance proposes, in accordance with similar cases for poor and unfortunate scholarship recipients, an annual support of 150 Gulden until Hölderlin recovers.

Annotation dated **12 October**: 'His Royal Majesty wishes that the ministry graciously grant Hölderlin the requested support of 150 Gulden until his recovery.'

**16 October.** 'The widow Gok in Nürtingen is hereby granted an annual support of 150 Gulden for the care of her ailing son until such date as he recovers.'

16 October, clinic records, in Kerner's handwriting:
As before

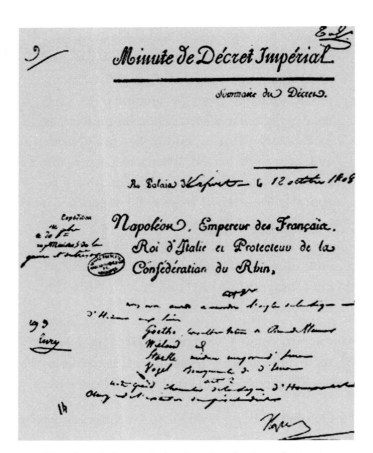

**9.** Napoleon's decree inducting Goethe into the Legion
of Honour, 12 October 1808.

17 October, in Autenrieth's handwriting:

| Gum of aloe, | 3 drams |
| | (1 dram = 3.654 grams) |
| Vitriolated tartar, | 3 drams |
| White sugar, | 3 ounces |
| Chamomile water with anise, | 3 ounces |
| Anise water, | 3 ounces |

One full tablespoon every two hours

These prescriptions follow the clinic's standard treatment protocol, where the section 'On Mania' reads:

> Belladonna or digitalis purpurea seem to stun the nervous system of the maniac, and this seems to have the consequence of aiding recovery . . . treatment with mercury, either alone or in connection with an external inflammation, causes fever and in this case drastic agents are indicated, i.e. the use of aloe or black hellebore . . . the constant use of suitable stimulants—coffee or wine—together with a little food soothes the mood and in a couple of days makes this seemingly dangerous state pass.

From clinic records dated 21 October:

'Hölderlin—strolling.'

# 1807

*7 February. From Goethe's diary: 'Read Newton's* Optics. *Visited his Most Serene Highness until his departure. After lunch Fernow came and brought four portraits . . . In the evening, Faniska.'*

*23 March. French troops enter Madrid.*

*29 March. Hegel publishes* The Phenomenology of Spirit.

*3 May. Letter from Goethe to Schmidt: 'You will receive three pieces from Herr Haide:* Egmont, Stella *and* The Enigma. *I hope you will be able to use them. Continued Swiss Journey. After lunch, Fernow and Dr Haberle. In the evening, Meyer, Voigt and his wife, and Falk for tea.'*

*23 May. From Goethe's diary:*

> *Eight o'clock, letter to Voigt. Reply to an express. The medallist Manfredini has sculpted a medal of Bodoni. Perhaps he is the same sculptor who made the medal of Napoleon after the battle of Jena. At ten o'clock I started dictating a new story. Lunch at Hendrick's. Afterwards he, Knebel, and I went to the battlefield of Jena. Drew four scenes of the battlefield.*

# 1807

Justinus Kerner, who later exhibited a growing interest in Hölderlin's poems, was an intern at Autenrieth's clinic. As the record of prescriptions shows, Kerner was charged with monitoring Hölderlin's condition. In a letter from early 1807, he hastily reports his impressions: 'Herr Hölderlin is still quite ill. I went to see him today, and he spoke of nothing but Con.flex and other confused things which saddened me to hear. It is therefore profoundly unfortunate that Weisser criticized him so harshly, denying him a degree of logic and reason he undoubtedly still had.'

The meaning of the term *Con.flex*—which Adolph Beck deciphered from Kerner's handwritten letter—remains unclear. Rejecting Beck's belief that it was a Latin reference, other scholars hypothesized that it was a misreading of the word *Conflux*, a term Autenrieth used to explain states of madness ('mania is almost always produced by the confluence [*der Conflux*] of psychic and physical causes'). Since it seems unlikely Autenrieth would have used this term when speaking with his patient, *Conflex* should be listed alongside *Pallaksh* and *wari* as the very first of the

*28 May.* Napoleon's army defeats the Bourbon army commanded by Louis, Landgrave of Hesse-Philippsthal at Mileto.

*14 June.* Napoleon defeats the Russian army at Friedland.

*7–9 July.* Napoleon signs a peace treaty with Tsar Alexander I and King Frederick William II of Prussia at Tilsitt.

*13–14 July.* From Goethe's diary:

> *Towards evening Herr von Mohrenheim, secretary of the Russian embassy, brought me Kleist's* Amphitryon. *I read it and marvelled at this singular sign of the times . . . The ancient treatment of* Amphitryon *was about mental confusion and a schism between thought and conviction . . . The present treatment, Kleist's, looks instead at the main characters' emotional confusion. Kleist's drama is nothing less than a Christian interpretation of the myth, an adumbration of Mary through the Holy Spirit, as in the scene between Zeus and Alcmena. But the end is lamentable. The real Amphitryon must be pleased that Zeus has done him this honour. As for the rest, Alcmena's situation is painful and Amphitryon's is, ultimately, cruel.*

meaningless terms with which Hölderlin surprised his visitors.

From Friedrich Weisser's review of Hölderlin's elegy *Herbstfeier* ('Autumn Festival'), published in Leo von Seckendorf's *Musenalmanach für das Jahr 1807*:

> Herr Hölderlin yet again, and still utterly in vain, struggles to express the inexpressible in his work. This collection opens with the poem 'Autumn Festival', which begins 'Yet another joy is experienced!' Clearly, Herr Hölderlin descends on occasion from his previous heights. That effusion, and the subsequent line 'Open once again is the hall, and healthy is the garden', have more to do with prose than with poetry. The valley said to be 'high and stormy with vegetation' is complete nonsense, and just where one is to seek out a 'kingdom of song', in which 'all the bound wings venture' only heaven and Herr Hölderlin know.

**7 February.** Seckendorf writes to Kerner:

> Hölderlin's fate is near and dear to me. How can he survive in this world without relationships, without adequate care, without the comfort and satisfaction friendship could offer his tormented heart? It is truly sad: lethal loneliness

*13 August.* Goethe writes from the baths at Karlsbad:

> Visited the castle spring with Councillor Becker, who told me about the initiatives of the Augusteum and several other medal-awarding councils . . . Later visited with Prince Solms, first at the castle spring, then at the Theresa spring. Then went to Müller's, who brought out some beautiful prints and fragments of grey stone from Lessau. Visit from Cramer: discussed various things about Vienna, its theatre, etc.

*28 August.* From Goethe's diary:

> The Broken Jug (*by Kleist*) has extraordinary merits, and the entire play violently imposes its presence. It is too bad that the work belongs to the genre of invisible theatre. The author's talent is capable of vivid representation, but tends too much towards the dialectical, as he himself has shown with this stationary mode of recitation. Had he managed to realize a true work of drama, and naturally as well as skilfully let the action unfold before our eyes and senses . . . it would have been a great gift to German theatre.

*Mid-September.* 'The Weimar theatre has hired an amiable tenor, which bodes well.'

and constant brooding have destroyed him. Please send him my warmest greetings, if he even remembers me—is he capable of showing any concrete awareness? He doesn't yet know that some of his poems have been published in the almanac, because when I wrote to Sinclair, I couldn't reach him.

**3 May.** Hölderlin is discharged from Autenrieth's clinic and entrusted to the care of Ernst Zimmer, a carpenter, and his wife, who give him a room in the garret of their house overlooking the Neckar. 'In the clinic . . . Hölderlin was getting worse and worse,' Zimmer wrote several years later.

> I had read his *Hyperion*, which I enjoyed enormously. I visited him at the clinic, and regretted that such a superbly beautiful, sovereign mind should go to ruin. Since the clinic could do nothing more for him, Autenrieth suggested that I take him in, since he could not imagine a more suitable place than my home. Hölderlin was and still is a great admirer of nature, and his room offered a view of the entire Neckar and Steinlach valleys.

Hölderlin lived in this house for the remaining 36 years of his life.

*26 October.* From *Goethe's diary:* 'Read *Schelling's speech "Über das Verhältnis der bildenden Künste zu der Natur"* [*On the Relation between the Visual Arts and Nature*]. *Walked and then visited Frau von Stein.*'

*27 October.* Napoleon and the Spanish prime minister meet in secret regarding the partition of Portugal under their domain.

The room on the upper floor of the tower, 'a small, whitewashed chamber shaped like an amphitheatre', burnt down in 1875. It has since been rebuilt—albeit with rounded walls, instead of its original, angular hexagonal shape—and can be visited. The view truly is stupendous.

**23 May.** Sinclair writes to Hegel, 'I've no news of Hölderlin, except that Dr Autenried [*sic*] is treating him in Tübingen—to what end I do not know. Seckendorf published a few of his works in the latest almanac; although Hölderlin wrote them in his current condition, I consider them incomparable. Schlegel and Tieck, with whom I spoke last year, also consider these works the highest of their kind in all modern poetry. I pray to God Hölderlin's fortune might change, once and for all!'

**13 August.** Seckendorf writes to Kerner:

Sinclair recently sent me a couple of Hölderlin's poems, asking after him with concern. I fear the poet is incurable! But he remains such an extraordinary man! So he hasn't forgotten *Aurora*. It's true that, over four years ago now, when I asked him to send some prose works for the magazine, he sent poems instead. Then I was

arrested, and *Aurora* ceased publication. We never discussed payment . . . .

**Summer–autumn.** According to Zimmer's subsequent account, after an initial period of crises, Hölderlin never caused him any difficulty. The initial phase was likely a result of the treatment he received at the clinic; according to Zimmer, 'so much blood would rise to his head that his face turned red as a brick, and everything seemed to offend him.' But that soon passed, and he went on to say:

> He has a noble heart and a deep soul, his body is perfectly healthy, and he never fell ill during his entire stay with me. His well-formed figure is in fine shape, and I have never seen eyes as beautiful as his in any other mortal . . . Hölderlin has no fixed ideas whatsoever; it may be that he has enriched his imagination to the detriment of his intellect.

## 1808

**4 January.** *Napoleon visits David's studio and admires the painting of his coronation.*

**4 February.** *French troops enter Spain, occupying Pamplona and Barcelona. Murat is named 'Lieutenant General of the Realm of the Kingdom of Spain'.*

**2 February.** *Pope Pius VII rejects the naval blockade imposed by Napoleon against England. The following day, French troops under the command of General Miollis enter Rome, and he is appointed governor.*

**11 April.** *From Goethe's diary:'Elective Affinities must be treated as a collection of short stories, although they do tend to go on and on; the subject matter is too deeply rooted in me . . . Spent noontime alone. Had dinner with Meyer . . . Talked mostly about my short stories.'*

**2 May.** *The people of Madrid rise up against the French and the insurrection spreads throughout Spain.*

**7 July.** *Joseph Bonaparte, whom Napoleon proclaimed King of Spain, is defeated by the rebels at Bailén and forced to withdraw from Madrid.*

# 1808

Hölderlin receives a piano, on which he improvises and plays at length, from memory, providing his own vocal accompaniment. He also resumes playing the flute.

From Waiblinger's biography (this description is from later years, but may well be relevant to this period as well):

> Hölderlin's days are extremely simple. In the mornings, especially in summertime, when he is agitated and tormented inside, he gets up before dawn or right as the sun rises and ventures out immediately, wandering around outside the house and in the courtyard. This walk usually lasts four or five hours, until he grows tired. He enjoys knocking his handkerchief against the fence posts and tearing up bits of grass. Whatever he finds, even the smallest piece of iron or leather, he puts in his pocket and keeps . . . Then he returns to the house and roams from room to room. He has a hearty appetite, and eats his meals in his room; he also enjoys wine, and would drink more if it were offered. After each meal he cannot bear for any

**1 August.** *Murat is proclaimed King of Naples.*

**1 October.** *Goethe and other dignitaries are invited to meet with Napoleon at the Congress of Erfurt.*

**2 October.** *Napoleon again summons Goethe to the Palace in Erfurt and receives him while dining with Talleyrand and Daru, his superintendent of finance. Speaking of fatalistic tragedy in the theatrical realm, Napoleon tells his guest, 'Why, today, do they keep giving us destiny? . . . Politics is destiny.' A few days later, he confers the Cross of the Legion of Honour on Goethe and Wieland.*

**3–17 October.** *French troops besiege Capri, still occupied by English troops. On 17 October the English surrender. Murat, in order to gain the favour of the Church, donates 1,600 ducats to the powerful parish of San Gennaro, thereby guaranteeing that the miracle of the holy blood's liquefaction will take place.*

**14–15 October.** *Goethe drafts a letter to Maret to thank the emperor for his induction into the Legion of Honour.*

Vôtre Excellence [comprendra] l'effet que sa lettre, qui m'annonce les hautes faveurs dont il a plu a sa Majesté l'Empereur de m'honorer, devait faire sur moi. Vôtre Excellence voudra vec sa bonté ordinaire accueillir les expressions dishes to remain inside his room, even for a moment, so he sets them on the floor outside his door. The only objects he tolerates in his room are his own belongings, everything else is set outside, in front of the door.

**15 October.** Hölderlin's mother writes her will, expressing worry about her ailing son's fate and begging her daughter and youngest son:

Disregard the sums your dear, pitiable brother has needed for his studies, his travel expenses as tutor, and during the course of his wretched illness—not least because I have benefitted from the inheritance received from his father longer than the inheritance left to my two other children ... Should the good Lord decide to leave my poor, sick son in this sad condition even after my death, in which case he will have no need of property, then my two other children shall inherit it, half each, as compensation. It is my hope that the interest, on top of what he receives annually, will suffice to meet all his needs, so that the poor dear will be fully taken care of. I therefore ask the honourable court and my two other children to see to it that my ailing son's capital is not touched, so faibles d'une reconnaissance respectueuse et profonde; Elle voudra se faire interprete vis à vis de sa Majesté des sentiments que je suis incapable d'articuler . . .

*Your Excellency must surely understand the effect that letter, announcing the high honours his Majesty the Emperor has seen fit to confer upon me, has had on me. I trust Your Excellency will be willing to accept, with his usual kindness, these faint expressions of my deepest and most respectful gratitude and, further, be willing to interpret for his Majesty the feelings I myself am incapable of expressing . . .*

*The next day, Goethe addresses Sartorius: '"Emperor Napoleon granted me the Legion of Honour, and Czar Alexander also gave me an honorific." As he said this, he showed us the parcel the butler had just brought, containing the large ribbon of the Order of Saint Anne with a glittering star. He then left to put it on, as he was invited to court to give a speech.'*

*5 November. Napoleon's Spanish campaign begins. Marshal Soult defeats the Spaniards in the battle of Gamonal and occupies Burgos.*

*4 December. Madrid surrenders, Napoleon orders the abolition of feudal rights and abolishes the tribunal of the*

that, after his death, they may receive what is
left in recompense . . . I further ask that, after
my death, my other two children act as father
and mother to their unfortunate brother.

**29 December.** The writer Karl August Varnhagen von
Ense accompanies Kerner on a visit to Hölderlin, and
leaves an account rife with inaccuracies and arbitrary
interpretations:

> Kerner led me to another poet—a poet in the
> truest sense of the word, an authentic master
> of poetry—although he can be found neither
> at court nor at Cotta's soirées, but solely in a
> lunatic asylum. I was shocked to learn that
> Hölderlin has been living here for two years
> as a veritable madman! The noble poet of
> the *Hyperion* and so many other magnificent,
> nostalgic, heroic works has also published a
> translation from Sophocles; I found it rather
> extravagant, but only in the literary sense,
> because here [in Germany] one can venture far
> indeed from the original without actually
> being insane or considered such. Faulting such
> extravagance was certainly legitimate, and, in
> addition to other characters, I had imagined a
> translator named Wachholder for this double

*Inquisition. He instructs Savary to requisition all silver and gold coinage and valuables.*

**29 December.** *From Goethe's diary: 'Simon Portius; discussed theatre with Genast. Spent midday alone. Continued discussing play direction with Genast after lunch.' Letter to Voigt: 'Thanks to Your Excellency's good disposition, we were able to please our employees in Jena.' Von Müller observes: 'I found Goethe stiff, abrupt, and heavy-handed. It was a gloomy, foggy day, a harbinger of the thaw!'*

**30 December.** *The fifth coalition against France is established.*

novel, who would speak like Hölderlin's Sophocles. It was only by chance that I did not, which turned out to work in my favour! I now shudder at the thought that I might have ended up mocking a mentally ill person, which would have been as shameful as beating a corpse . . . Poor Hölderlin! He is entrusted to the care of a carpenter, who feeds him, treats him well, walks with him, and keeps an eye on him—his madness is not at all dangerous, as long as he doesn't pay too much attention to the ideas that suddenly spring into his head. He isn't delirious, but speaks incessantly, voicing a vivid imagination, and apparently believes he is surrounded by visitors paying him homage; he argues with them, listens to their objections, and contradicts them with great vivacity. He also quotes from the great works he has written, and others he is currently writing; all his knowledge, his skilful facility with language, and his familiarity with ancient authors are still present—rarely, however, does his speaking reveal any genuine thought or logical connection, since his stream of words is for the most part complete nonsense. Apparently, the cause of his madness was a star-crossed sojourn in Frankfurt, where he

was a tutor for a rich family. A tender, amiable and unhappy lady developed an appreciation for the poet's high mind, for the pure soul of the despondent and misunderstood young man, and an innocent friendship was born. However, the coarsest suspicions were nevertheless aroused, and both Hölderlin and his friend were horrifically mistreated! This broke his heart. He tried to bury his pain by devoting himself to his work on Sophocles. The publisher, who released the first part, did not realize that there were already signs of his decline in that book, which unfortunately soon became visible in the author himself.

## 1809

*1 January. Cambacérès informs Napoleon that Austria is mobilizing its troops.*

*10 January. Goethe writes a letter to the Royal Theatre of Weimar instructing its leaders to remedy the 'decadent state of masked balls'* (Verfall der Redouten).

> *The curtains of the Estrade should remain open, so that high-ranking people and the haute bourgeoisie may linger there, playing games or conversing. Ideally, a court usher will be present, to make the necessary introductions.*
>
> *No one may enter in everyday attire. Should attendees not wish to choose a mask and appear in character, they may don a black cloak or Domino.*
>
> *Dancing in boots is not permitted.*

*12 April. Austria declares war on France.*

*28 April. Goethe writes a letter to the Royal Theatre of Weimar: 'His Most Serene Highness expressed to me his wish to see the actor Schwarz cast in* Lorenz Stark, *and did so in a way I could not refuse. The theatrical commission shall, therefore, kindly see to it.'*

## 1809

**Early April.** Uhland and Kerner visit Hölderlin.

**6 May.** Leo von Seckendorf, captaining the Austrian troops, perishes while fighting the French at the Battle of Ebelsberg.

**6 July.** Jacob Zwilling, a friend of Sinclair's whom Hölderlin had frequented at Jena, dies in the Battle of Wagram.

**8 September.** Karl Philipp Conz, Hölderlin's friend from their student days in Tübingen, suggests to August Mahlmann, publisher of the Leipzig-based *Zeitung für die elegante Welt*, that he publish a collection of writings Hölderlin's family had entrusted to him. 'I am in possession of several unpublished texts—both poetry and prose—by Hölderlin, my friend and fellow countryman. You are undoubtedly aware of his talent, although he has unfortunately been in an altered mental state for many years now. He has been retired for some time, and his condition seems incurable.' Since Conz believes 'the current state of the book trade' would make it inadvisable to publish a collection strictly composed

*6 May.* Goethe writes a letter to Eichstädt: 'Would Your Lordship have the courtesy to arrange for the librarian to come by each morning at nine o'clock to collect the books I've finished with and take note of my new requests?'

*13 May.* After a month-long campaign, French troops enter Vienna.

*6 July.* Goethe writes a letter to Sartorius:

> This work by Mariotte fills an important gap in the key period that I, too, am now working with. I aim to show, historically, how Newton first acted hastily, and then persisted; why his opponents, although they were largely right, were unable to prevail over him; and how his equally thoughtless, prejudiced and obstinate school of thought took hold and spread worldwide . . .

From Goethe's diary: 'Spent midday with Kaaz. Towards evening saw Frau Wolzogen and Madame Councillor von Schiller. Otherwise alone. Prepared various things.'

*8 September.* From Goethe's diary: 'Sixth chapter of Elective Affinities and a few other things. After lunch, Schlegel's lecture on Greek comedy.' This same day, Goethe writes a letter to Christiane Vulpius: 'I would very much like to see you and speak with you, but we're in such an urgent of poems, he proposes a selection combining earlier poems which 'stand out for their warmth and intimacy' with more recent pieces, which 'bear the marks of excessive complexity, idealized refinement, and a highly mannered, Grecianizing style'. Alongside the poems, Conz suggests an excerpt of 'nearly two acts' from the iambic drama *Empedocles* and a prose essay 'on the different directions of poetry', which 'contains many sharp insights expressed in a lively, harmonious style, even if I cannot say I entirely agree with the author'. After inquiring about potential payment, Conz further stipulates that Hölderlin's name not appear on the final publication: 'Despite his altered mental state, he still has an obsessive desire [*die Grille*] to control all edits of his own work. If he learns that something of his had been published without his knowledge . . . he is always very annoyed and rails against unauthorized infringement of his rights.'

The fact that Hölderlin's ongoing desire to oversee any publication of his own work was considered an absurd, extravagant demand eloquently demonstrates how even his most well-intentioned friends now regarded even his most legitimate, reasonable requests a sign of pure folly.

situation with OUR WORK that I'd rather you not come just yet, as we must make every hour count, and I don't see how we'll manage to finish . . . I'm doing quite well but am following a strict diet and orderly way of life . . . Evening at home. Prints of Italian scenes by Huber and Füessli.'

**13 October.** Friedrich Staps, an eighteen-year-old German, attempts to assassinate Napoleon at Schönbrunn.

**20–21 October.** From Goethe's diary:

> Drafted a biographical outline. Went for a walk in the eastern part of the region . . . Spent the evening with Meyer: art history, numismatics and gems . . . Strolled with August to Belvedere Castle. Visited the castle with Herr von Hinzenstern. On the way back, saw the Crown Prince and then His Highness. Later went home. Evening at the theatre: Bluebeard.

**15 December.** Napoleon divorces Joséphine in preparation for his subsequent marriage to Marie Louise of Austria.

**20 October.** Mahlmann replies that he'd happily publish the proposed collection, but can only offer 10 thalers per page, a sum 'certainly lower than what Cotta [Goethe's publisher] could pay ... I agree with you that Hölderlin's name should not appear, since other unscrupulous people have released so much of his work that would have best remained unpublished, thereby tarnishing his name. The first part of the *Hyperion* is the height of his genius, but after that he got lost in formalism and incomprehensible profundity.'

The proposed collection was never published.

**1 January.** Kerner informs Heinrich Köstlin, a friend from Tübingen, that he is writing a piece titled *Reiseschatten*, which will 'also feature Hölderlin'.

**21 January.** In a letter to Otto Runge, Clemens Brentano mentions the 'deep impression' made on him by

certain odes of the mad poet from Württemberg, Hölderlin—such as his elegy to the night, 'Autumn Festival', 'The Rhine', 'Patmos', and others—which were forgotten and ignored in Seckendorf's two *Musenal-manachen* in 1807 and 1808. Never before, I believe, has such a highly contemplative pain been expressed so magnificently. Sometimes this genius darkens, and sinks into the bitter springs of his heart; but more often his moving, apocalyptic star shines magnificently upon his vast sea of sensitivity. If you can find these books, read these poems. In particular, his elegy to the night is clear and shining as a star; it is also lonely, like a bell whose tolling is triggered by each and every memory: I consider it one of the most successful poems.

**16 August.** Sinclair, in Homburg, writes to Hegel about Zwilling's death at Wagram, adding: 'I've heard nothing more of poor Hölderlin ... I suppose his situation hasn't changed, but do tell me if you have any news.' The letter shows how detached Sinclair had become from his old friend: despite having 'heard nothing more' of Hölderlin, he considered—perhaps in an act of subconscious self-justification—his madness incurable.

# 1811

**7 January.** August Mayer, a student also boarding with the Zimmer family, writes to his brother:

> Poor Hölderlin wants to publish an almanac, and writes several pages every day. Today he gave me a whole folder to read; I'll transcribe a few passages for you. The following is the end of a beautiful poem on death of a child:

> *Die Schönheit ist den Kindern eigen,*
> *Ist Gottes Ebenbild vielleicht,*
> *Ihr Eigentum ist Ruh und Schweigen,*
> *Das Engeln auch zum Lob gereicht.*

> Beauty belongs to the children,
> 'tis perhaps the likeness of God,
> they possess a peace and silence,
> which earns even angels' homage.

And here are some amusing lines from a poem titled 'Der Ruhm' ('Fame'):

> *Es knüpft an Gott der Wohllaut, der geleitet*
> *Ein sehr berühmtes Ohr, den wunderbar*
> *Ist ein berühmtes Leben gross und klar,*

*So geht der Mensch zu Fusse oder reitet.*
*Der Erde Freuden, Freundlichkeit und Güter,*
*Der Garten, Baum, der Weinberg mit dem Hüter,*
*Sie scheinen mir ein Wiederglanz des Himmels*
*Gewähret von dem Geist den Söhnen des Gewimmels.*
*Wenn Einer ist mit Gütern reich beglücket,*
*Wenn Obst den Garten ihm, und Gold ausschmücket*
*Die Wohnung und das Haus, was mag er haben*
*Noch mehr in dieser Welt, sein Herz zu laben?*

From God come the dulcet words that aim
At very famous ears; for 'tis indeed
Both grand and simple, to lead a life of fame,
Whether one walks or rides a steed.
All worldly pleasures, friendliness and goods,
The garden, the tree, the vineyard and its keeper,
All strike me as a reflection of heaven that
The holy spirit grants our ever-teeming sons.
If a man is blessed with goods unfurled,
If fruits adorn his orchard, if his home and hearth
are decked in gold, what more in the world
Could he ever desire to satisfy his heart?

And on the birth of a child:

*Wie wird des Himmels Vater schauen*
*Mit Freude das erwachs'ne Kind,*

*Gehend auf blumenreichen Auen,*
*Mit andern, welche lieb ihm sind.*
*Indessen freue dich des Lebens,*
*Aus einer guten Seele kommt*
*Die Schönheit herrlichen Bestrebens,*
*Gottlicher Grund dir mehr noch frommt.*

How will Heavenly Father look after,
With such delight the grown child
Walking through wildflower pastures,
With others, grown dear, as they whiled.
Meantime, take joy that you are living,
From a true soul there issues forth
The beauty of noble striving,
Divine reason grants even greater worth.

These verses moved me: 'The world's comforts I've savoured . . . '.

*Das Angenehme dieser Welt hab' ich genossen,*
*Die Jugenstunden sind, wie lang! wie lang! verflossen,*
*April und Mai und Julius sind ferne*
*Ich bin nichts mehr, ich lebe nicht mehr gerne!*

The world's comforts I've savoured, and held fast
But youthful days are now long, long past
April and May and July are long gone
I'm nothing now, I don't wish to live on.

**21 January.** Kerner writes to Friedrich de la Motte Fouqué,

> Do you know our country's poet Hölderlin? He still writes poems—despite his ruinous state, his madness—although they're mostly incomprehensible. But today a friend sent me these moving verses, apparently found among his papers, which are perfectly comprehensible:
>
> '*Das Angenehme dieser Welt hab' ich genossen* . . .
>
> 'Varnhagen knows him personally. Please transcribe these verses for him, because I don't know where he lives.'

In late January, Kerner publishes a booklet in Heidelberg titled *Reiseschatten. Von dem Schattenspieler Luchs.* The story's characters include a chemist, a parish priest, a carpenter and a mad poet named Holder, evidently inspired by Hölderlin. The text has an obviously satirical, irreverent tone:

> As soon as he recognized me, my friend Holder embraced me with great affection and said: ' 'Tis doubly happy that I should meet you here, in this town, on your journey northward: for at the confluence of star and song, where the dinner chalice soars like a comet across the sky,

a sea is born, the sea of the north, and iron is born upon it—and from the north, the unfulfilled shall come: for iron points northward, as does its spirit, the magnet.' At this point he was seized with ecstatic convulsions, and added: 'Grant me the metallic spirit of the earth, and its eye of gold! Do not tear your limbs asunder by allowing an insolent populace to proliferate! Ha ha ha! That's how I want to live my entire life, altogether!'

It's no surprise that, when Mayer showed Zimmer this text, the latter recognized the carpenter as a parody of himself, tossed the book onto the table, and exclaimed:

Whoever wrote this would've been better off working in the fields, rather than scribbling such rubbish . . . idiocy is idiocy, and can even be forgiven, but portraying others from life— and I don't mean me, I'm irrelevant here, but to spoof a poor madman like Hölderlin—is utterly foolish and reveals the author's absolutely immoral character.

**14 October.** Zimmer writes to Hölderlin's mother:

Yesterday I ventured out again with your dear son, who stood under my father's plum tree and laughed heartily when someone shook it and a bunch of plums fell on his head. On the way home, we ran into Professor Konz [*sic*], who greeted your son, calling him *Herr Magister*.Your son immediately replied, 'You call me Herr Magister—', and Konz apologized, saying 'It doesn't matter what titles we old acquaintances give one another' [*wie wir uns titulieren*]. He then took a volume by Homer out of his pocket and said, 'You see, I have our old friend with me.' Hölderlin looked up a passage and gave it to Konz to read, and Konz enthusiastically read it, which enchanted your son. Konz then said, 'Farewell, Herr Librarian', and this made your son very happy. But just three days later he had a violent outburst, insistently shouting, 'I am no *magister*, I am the prince's librarian!' He stormed out, and sulked for a long time, but now he's once again completely calm.

# 1812

**5 February.** In a letter to Hegel, Sinclair recalls 'the pact between our spirits, although destiny has torn it asunder', and the days spent with Hölderlin and Zwilling, which 'shall forever remain unforgettable'.

**19 April.** Zimmer writes to Hölderlin's mother:

Most honourable Madam Councillor,

Your dear Hölderle [*sic*] has undergone a note-worthy change, his body has been growing slimmer for some time now, although he has a greater appetite than usual. Over the last four months he has been calmer than usual, and even when seized by a paroxysm he didn't pant much and generally got over it swiftly.

But about ten days ago he grew restless during the night, and began pacing around in my workshop, talking to himself. I got up and asked him how he was feeling, but he begged me to go to back to bed and leave him alone. Utterly lucid, he said: 'I can't stay in bed, I have to walk, you can rest assured I won't do anything to anyone, go back to sleep, my dear

Zimmer.' Then he cut off the conversation, and I had no choice but to go to bed again lest I irritate him, so I let him do as he wished.

By morning he was calm, but was very hot to the touch and thirsty, like someone with a strong fever and chills. He grew so weak that he took to bed, and by midnight he was sweating profusely.

On the second day he was even hotter to the touch, and thirstier, and then he sweat so much that the bed and everything he was wearing was completely drenched. This lasted for a few more days, then a rash appeared on his mouth, and although his temperature, thirst, and sweat gradually disappeared, his shivers unfortunately remained, strong, but not as strong as before. Now he's been out of bed again all day and expresses himself politely. His gaze is friendly, even amiable, and he plays music and sings and is very reasonable. The most remarkable thing is that, since that night, he has had no trace of restlessness, whereas previously he'd have at least an hour of restlessness each day. Even the smell in his room, which was so strong, especially in the morning, has disappeared.

I called medical Professor Gmelin, as a doctor for your dear son, and he couldn't issue any precise prognosis regarding your son's state. He believes it is a consequence of nature alone, and unfortunately, dear Madam, I am in the sad position of having to write that I concur . . .

His poetic spirit is perpetually active; he saw a drawing of a temple at my place and asked me to build him one out of wood. I replied that I have to earn my daily bread, I'm not as fortunate as he, and cannot afford to live in philosophical peace, to which he replied 'Oh, I am a poor man', and within the next minute he took a pencil and wrote these verses on a board:

*Die Linien des Lebens sind verschieden*
*wie Wege sind, und wie der Berge Gränzen.*
*Was hir sind, kann dort ein Gott ergänzen*
*mit Harmonien und ewigem Lohn und Frieden.*

The lines of life are varied and contrasting
Much like paths, or bounded mountain lands.
All that is here, a God there can expand on
With harmonies, reward, and peace everlasting.

As for his room and board, you can rest assured. The final days of my wife's pregnancy went well, and she was able to take care of your son herself. She gave birth the day before yesterday. Unfortunately, the baby died within a few hours but, thank God, she is well and out of danger.

I am enclosing the bill for your son; we now have to heat his room all the time, since he easily gets a chill, so we had to buy more wood. He's having coffee again at breakfast, and then we cook him a meal of his own.

| Expenses for 81 days | 32 Gulden and 24 Kreuzers |
|---|---|
| 69 glasses of wine | 6 F. 54 K. |
| snuff | 1.21 |
| wood | 3.18 |
| laundry | 3 |
| lighting, all winter | 1.36 |
| | 48.33 |
| minus | 6 |
| | 42.33 |

Your devoted servant, Ernst Zimmer

**15 September.** Hölderlin writes to his mother:

My esteemed Mother,

I am most honoured to state that I was very pleased with the letter I received from you.

Your excellent expressions are of great benefit to me, and to the gratitude I already owe you I must now add my deep admiration for your excellent intentions. You never fail to express your benevolent spirit and useful admonitions in such a way that causes me to both rejoice and put them into practice. The clothing you sent also suits me very well. I must make haste but allow me to take the liberty of adding one final observation: your recommendation that I maintain my orderly conduct shall, I hope, be both effective and appreciated by you.

May I be so honoured as to call myself

your most affectionate son

Hölderlin

(The exaggerated formality of this letter is characteristic of Hölderlin's communication with the outside world. The fact that it is a conscious, almost parodic way of distancing himself from his interlocutors is particularly evident in his correspondence with his mother, who consistently expressed complete incomprehension of her son's aspirations; indeed, one of her 'excellent intentions' was that he devote his energies to becoming a parish priest.)

# 1813

Early in the year, Hölderlin writes to his mother:

My esteemed Mother,

I should like to take advantage of Herr Zimmer's generous offer to send you my thoughts and entertain you yet again by reaffirming my dedication to you and the sincerity of my affection. Your clear goodness, which has enlightened me for so long, and your ongoing tenderness and moral influence, which are so beneficial to me, are exemplary. I always keep them in mind, whether aiming to express all due respect or contemplating the commemoration I owe you, excellent mother! If I am unable to entertain you as pleasantly as you entertain me, it is due to the implicit self-negation [*das Verneinende*] inherent in my self-same devotion [*ebenderselber Ergebenheit*] to you. My admiration of you remains strong; how enduring is your goodness, how unchanged is my memory of you, venerable mother! I treasure each day that passes without harm to you and your health, and with the certainty of your heart of pleasing God, and the hours I have spent near you are, as I see it [*wie mir scheinet*], unforgettable. I hope and firmly trust that you will always fare well, and that you will take pleasure in this world. I am honoured to call myself [*nenne mich*]

Your devoted son

Hölderlin

(This letter, like the next, is a masterpiece of irony. It's worth noting that Hölderlin makes a point of underlining his name in his letters to his mother. At the same time, he mercilessly expresses his disapproval of her attitude towards him—note the singular expression *das Verneinende*—thinly veiling it under a layer of empty ceremoniousness. The reason he finds the hours spent with her unforgettable is suggested by the incongruous *wie mir scheinet*. In general, many elements of Hölderlin's behaviour previously attributed to madness can be read as the result of a subtle, calculated irony.)

**30 January.** Fouqué replies to a letter in which Kerner had sent him some of Hölderlin's poems, 'My best and most heartfelt thanks for Hölderlin's poems. They have gladdened my whole soul, and shall appear in a forthcoming collection titled *Frauentaschenbuch*.'

**2 March.** Zimmer writes to Hölderlin's mother:

Hölderlin is well behaved and consistently happy. The pipe chambers you so kindly sent cheered him up. He recognized them, and told me, 'I bought them in Frankfurt.' Then he added, 'In Frankfurt I needed a lot of money, but not nearly as much for my trip.' Whatever happens, you can rest assured we will look after your dear son. His stockings aren't yet so worn as to require mending. As far as I know, he lacks nothing . . .

I remain your devoted servant, Ernst Zimmer.

PS: I asked Hölderlin if he would like to write to you as well, but he doesn't seem to want to.

Later in the year, Hölderlin writes to his mother again:

My esteemed Mother,

I reply to your good letter with a glad heart and out of due [*schuldiger*] concern for your well-being, health and lifespan. When you instruct me—exhorting me to adhere to honest conduct, virtue and religion—the sweetness of such a good mother, both the understood and mysterious aspects of such a venerable relationship, is as useful to me as a good book, and as beneficial to my soul as the highest doctrine. The sheer naturalness of your pious, virtuous soul warrants better comparisons; I count on your Christian forgiveness, dearest mother, and on my perennial aspiration to improve upon myself. Until my soul is so enriched with wisdom that it may better express itself in words and be of some interest to you, my ability to communicate shall remain limited to expressing my affectionate dependence [*Anhänglichkeit*] on you. I take the liberty of asking your devout maternal heart to look after me, and of commending your constant excellence. I believe that your zeal and steady progress towards all that is good will meet their objective. I salute you, most venerable mother, and remain most sincerely

your devoted son

Hölderlin

# 1814

**22 February.** Zimmer writes to Hölderlin's mother:

Most honourable Lady Councillor,

I received your recent letter with the latest four-month payment . . .Your dear Hölderle is so well behaved, one couldn't hope for better. He was very pleased with his Christmas present—the jacket isn't too wide, if anything it's a little short. He was also very happy about the letter from the parish priest in Löschgau. He said, 'That man showed me a great deal of kindness when I was young.' He was also very pleased with the book by Böhlendorff, exclaiming, 'Ah! That fine man died early; he was from Curland. I met him in Homburg, and he really was a good friend.' I have to say that your dear Hölderle no longer has restless bouts, he is peaceful and contented. My little boy has started playing the piano, and your dear son often enjoys playing the piano, too. He can follow a score when he wants to, but he usually prefers to improvise, following his imagination . . .

**1 October.** Clemens Brentano writes to Rahel Varnhagen: 'If you have not yet read Hölderlin's *Hyperion* (Cotta, 1797), do so as soon as possible; it is one of the most remarkable books in our country— indeed, in the entire world.'

Hölderlin writes to his mother twice over the course of the year:

My esteemed Mother,

I do not believe it is burdensome that I repeat myself in these letters. Your tenderness and superb goodness reawaken my gratitude, and gratitude is a virtue. I think often of the time I spent with you, esteemed mother, and recognize its importance. The virtuous, unforgettable example you set shall remain with me at a distance [*in der Entfernung*], encouraging me to follow your directives and imitate your comportment.

I profess my sincere dedication, and remain

Your most devoted son

Hölderlin

Please send my dear sister my greetings.

(The mention of distance acquires an ironic tinge when one remembers that Hölderlin's mother never once visited her son in Tübingen.)

My esteemed Mother,

I consider myself fortunate to have so many opportunities to express my dedication to you in writing. I think I can say that good thoughts, expressed in words, are not in vain, because human sentiment is also shaped by inner laws that are inherent in human nature. Their constancy and benefits make them interesting, insofar as they express Christian values. Human beings seem to readily grow accustomed to reliability, a purity that apparently suits their inclinations. Such intimacy also seems to possess great strength, since it can help placate and empower the human soul. Divinity, to the extent that human beings are capable of accepting it, is marvellously granted a degree of attention that is more natural than that of humankind. I ask your forgiveness for speaking so carelessly. However serious it may appear, a disposition for taking care of oneself is sustained by the human spirit; due to the inclinations of the heart, it can also make life milder, thereby making one more sensitive. Once again, I must ask your forgiveness for ending my letter so abruptly. I remain, with the sincerest dedication,

your devoted son

Hölderlin

# 1815

**29 April.** Sinclair unexpectedly dies during the Congress of Vienna. There is no record of how Hölderlin reacted to the news.

Hölderlin's reputation as 'the poet in the garret' grows among university students in Tübingen. Arnim and Brentano continue to take an interest in his work.

**March.** Arnim writes:

> If one were to count up all the great German spirits who have sunk into illness, succumbed to suicide, or been felled by odious occupations, it would be a terrifying list indeed! Hölderlin expressed it best in his *Hyperion*: 'Where a people loves the beautiful, where it honours the genius in its artists, there blows like the breath of life a universal spirit, the bashful mind unfolds, self-conceit melts away, and all hearts are pious and great, and inspiration brings forth heroes. The homeland of all men is with such a people and there the stranger loves to linger. But where divine nature and its artists are so abused, oh! there life's greatest joy is gone, and any other star is better than the earth. There, all men, though

born beautiful, become ever wilder and more wasted; a servile disposition grows and with it rude courage; intemperance grows with cares, and with opulence hunger and fear of famine; each year's blessing becomes a curse and all the gods take flight.' This wonderful man, too, fell so ill, and grew so poor, that he went mad; he lives but is lost to us, for whom his pain in such dark times opened our hearts and freed our souls from the grip of need.

**18 April.** Hölderlin writes to his mother:

My esteemed Mother,

If my previous letters failed to please you completely, perhaps more frequent attention will convey my good intentions. This, too, can be a form of exercise. The exercise of habit [*zur Gewohnheit*] brings people together, and their ways of thinking and relationships also come together within the broader context of humanity. And yet the ways of thinking that remain closest take the form of gratitude, religion, and committed relationships. I remain devoted to your ongoing goodness and am, sincerely,

your devoted son

Hölderlin

**8 July.** Gustav Schwab writes in his diary:

Later on Brentano arrived, but he remained
silent until we set off with Savigny, who had
to fetch his wife. Along the road lined with
lindens he gave free rein to his wit, his spirited
self, but also to his unbridled impudence. He
demolished every poet except Shakespeare and
his own brother-in-law, Arnim. In his opinion,
Goethe is too classical and contrived, as is
Uhland, although the latter has some qualities;
Tieck, initially alluring, is a scoundrel of mod-
est intellect who forces his friends to worship
him and had a falling out with Goethe because
he cannot compete with his fame ... Arnim—
once again, his own brother-in-law—apparently has more wit and poetry in his pinkie
finger than Tieck has in his entire puffed-up
figure. Back when Brentano was a student in
Jena, and saw Tieck for the first time, he wept
with respect; and when the two Schlegels
walked down the street with Tieck in the
middle, he felt as if he had witnessed God the
Father, the Son, and the Holy Spirit strolling
by. Now he sees things rather differently, and
his highest ideal is Hölderlin.

Hölderlin writes to his mother (undated letter, possibly from the beginning of 1816):

> My esteemed Mother,
>
> Here I am writing another letter to you. You surely remember what I have written so often before, using nearly identical expressions. I hope you are well and will continue to be well. I send my most devoted greetings and remain
>
> > your devoted son
> >
> > Hölderlin

**28 January.** Arnim writes to Savigny: 'Poor is the mouth of the people, says Hölderlin, but even when our mouths are full, we have so very little to say.'

Later in the year, Hölderlin writes to his mother again:

> My esteemed Mother,
>
> As you know, I will always gladly write to you. You are aware of what I have become, and I habitually feel that my way of making myself comprehensible is as it must be. Please continue

to write me letters which require that I reply
with all due courtesy. I remain

your devoted son
Hölderlin

**December.** Brentano writes to Luise Hensel:

> I am now reminded of the loveliest poem I
> know. It is the only poem by this poet that
> exerts a magical violence on me; it brings me
> peace, and makes me feel as if the heavens have
> opened overhead, and I lie below this wide
> sky like a child on its mother's lap . . . I shall
> transcribe this poem for you . . . 'Night' by
> Hölderlin:

(*Brod und Wein*, lines 1–17)

*Rings um ruhet die Stadt; still wird die erleuchtete*
  *Gasse,*
*Und, mit Fackeln geschmückt, rauschen die Wagen*
  *hinweg.*
*Satt gehen von Freuden des Tags zu ruhen die*
  *Menschen,*
*Und Gewinn und Verlust wäget ein sinniges Haupt*
*Wohlzufrieden zu Haus; leer steht von Trauben und*
  *Blumen,*
*Und von Werken der Hand ruht der geschäftige Markt.*

*Aber das Saitenspiel tönt fern aus Gärten; vielleicht,*
*    dass*
*Dort ein Liebendes spielt oder ein einsamer Mann*
*Ferner Freunde gedenkt und der Jugendzeit; und die*
*    Brunnen*
*Immerquillend und frisch rauschen an duftendem Beet.*
*Still in dämmriger Luft ertönen geläutete Glocken,*
*Und der Stunden gedenkt rufet ein Wächter die Zahl.*
*Jetzt auch kommet ein Wehn und regt die Gipfel des*
*    Hains auf,*
*Sieh! und das Schattenbild unserer Erde, der Mond,*
*Kommet geheim nun auch; die Schwärmerische, die*
*    Nacht kommt,*
*Voll mit Sternen dort, die Fremdlingin unter den*
*    Menschen,*
*über Gebirgeshöhn traurig und prächtig herauf.*

Round about the city rests. The illuminated
    streets
Grow quiet, and coaches adorned with torches
    rush by.
Sated on the day's pleasures, everyone goes home
    to rest,
Gains and losses are tallied by clever minds
Back home, contented. Emptied of grapes and
    flowers

and handicrafts, the bustling marketplace grows
    silent.
But the music of strings resounds in distant
    gardens, where
Perhaps lovers are carousing, or a lonely man is
    thinking
Of faraway friends and his own youth. Fountains'
Flowing waters pass by fragrant flowerbeds,
Bells softly ring through the twilight and a
    watchman,
Mindful of the time, announces the hour.
Now a breeze also rises and caresses the grove's
    crown—
Look! The moon, shadow of our earth,
Is also stealthily rising. Impassioned Night is
    upon us,
Star-filled, so foreign to humankind,
Sad yet splendorous, shining o'er the
    mountaintops.

## 1817

**27 February.** Kerner writes to Uhland and, referring to poets' abject poverty, quotes Hölderlin's poem 'The Journey' [*Die Wanderung*], which Seckendorf had published in the 1807 *Musenalmanach*. 'We shall see—we shall all have to accompany Hölderlin to the Caucasus.'

The lines he refers to:

*Ich aber will dem Kaukasos zu!*
*Denn sagen hört ich*
*Noch heut in den Lüften:*
*Frei sei'n, wie Schwalben, die Dichter.*

But it's the Caucasus I long for!
Just today I heard
The breezes say:
Poets must be free as birds.

Later in the year, Hölderlin writes to his mother:

Most esteemed Mother,

Please don't think ill of me if I always bother you with such short letters. Conveying one's own intentions and the interest one takes in others whom one adores and seeking to hear how their life is going—I feel a need to apologize for this mode of communication.

I must conclude here, but remain,

your devoted son

Hölderlin

## 1818

Two letters from Hölderlin to his mother:

Dearest Mother,

Since Herr Zimmer so kindly allows me to write you, I feel free to do so. I entrust myself to your goodness. You certainly won't abandon me. I hope to see you soon. From the bottom of my heart, I remain

your devoted son
Hölderlin

My esteemed Mother,

Here I am, writing to you again. The repetition of what one has written is not always an unnecessary engagement. It is founded in the nature of the matter that if one is exhorting oneself to good, and saying something serious, it will not be taken amiss if one repeats what they've said before and doesn't always come up with something out of the ordinary. I shall content myself with that. I present my compliments to you with great devotion and remain

your devoted son
Hölderlin

# 1819

Two letters from Hölderlin to his mother:

My esteemed Mother,
The excellent Frau Zimmer urges me not to neglect my duty of writing you to express my ongoing devotion. The duties people are bound to perform include a son's devotion to his mother. Human relations are bound by rules—practising and following these rules makes them seem less harsh, and better suited to one's heart. Please accept and be content with this sign of my lasting devotion.
I remain

your devoted son
Hölderlin

My esteemed Mother,
I take the liberty of writing you once more. What I have already said, I repeat again, with the knowledge that you already know. I wish you all the best. Forgive my brevity. I present my compliments to you with great devotion and remain

your devoted son
Hölderlin

# 1820

**10 May.** Kerner writes to Karl Mayer recommending that he

> collect and publish, for the benefit and honour of the entire country, Hölderlin's poems. It's a pity indeed that he, the sole elegiac poet in all Württemberg, should remain so forgotten, buried below the scrap heap of that carpenter in Tübingen. I cannot publish them myself, as I do not have the almanacs and magazines in which his poems previously appeared on hand. Haug and Neuffer would be best . . . Talk to Schwab, because he could also do it, or ask the right person to.

**29 August.** Sinclair's friend Heinrich von Dienst, a lieutenant infantryman, suggests that Cotta publish a collection of Hölderlin's poems and reissue *Hyperion*:

> Thanks to the late, covert advisor Sainclair [*sic*], I find myself in possession of a manuscript of six printed pages of poems by Friedrich Hölderlin, the author of *Hyperion*, some of which have appeared in various journals but others, as far as I know, have yet to be published.

Sainclair had intended to properly publish the poems of his poor friend and following his death it became my intention to do so as well, but the war and various other factors—in particular, my complete lack of knowledge regarding the author's situation and close relations—prevented me from doing so. I don't even know if he is still alive or living in the same old sorry state in Tübingen, or if he has relatives who might add any other work to a small collection, and ultimately publish it.

The proposal lists 33 poems, including 'Patmos', 'Der Rhein', 'Andenken', 'Hälfte des Lebens', 'Die Herbstfeyer' ('Herbstfeier'), 'Die Wanderung' and 'Blödigkeit'. The stated goal of this collection is to prevent 'a spirit like Hölderlin's from being swiftly forgotten, or even disappearing from our literature altogether'. Dienst proposes a preface by Johannes Schulze, Winckelmann's publisher, and the patronage of 'Her Royal Highness Princess Wilhelm of Prussia', to whom Hölderlin had dedicated his translation of *Antigone*.

Hölderlin writes to his mother:

My esteemed Mother,

Thank you for your recent letter. Based on what you wrote, I feel reassured that you are in good health and living a contented existence. Since you asked me how I believe I should behave towards you, I shall reply that I will do my best to stay on good terms with you. I remain,

your devoted son

Hölderlin

**7 September.** Cotta accepts Dienst's proposal. Meanwhile, Dienst has found other Hölderlin manuscripts among his papers, and sets out to find more works for the collection.

**25 September.** Dienst replies to Cotta:

As soon as I am in possession of the entire Hölderlin bequest, I shall do my best to arrange each piece according to the chronological order in which it appeared ...As soon as I have done so, High Councillor Schulze will kindly see to the proofreading, oversee the preface, and then send you the manuscript. As for the title of this collection, and whether it should be combined with *Hyperion* and published as a single volume, let's discuss and come to an agreement on that later.

**21 October.** Haug writes to Kerner, presumably after being informed of the latter's publication plans, to say that he believes 'Hölderlin would find it painful if someone else were to edit and publish his poems while he is still alive'—which is precisely how the poet subsequently reacts when, six years later, the proposed collection was published.

## 1821

**10 March.** Dienst writes to Kerner to inform him of the project and asks that, if he happens to have any other poems by Hölderlin, to 'kindly let me know, and tell me in which journals his previously published poems can be found'. Kerner writes Uhland later that same month, lamenting that 'a foreigner [*Ausländer*]' was in charge of the publication:' 'Tis a pity that a foreigner is now handling the work of our poor fellow citizen.' Kerner then contacts Hölderlin's half-brother, Karl Gok (whom the poet had always considered a brother), and Conz to suggest they take over the job: 'Certainly,' he writes to Gok, 'you must wish to assume the task of editing and publishing this work, for which we are so deeply indebted to our homeland and our dear friend.'

Hölderlin writes to his mother:

My esteemed Mother,

I am writing to you because I believe you'd want as much, and I wish to comply. If you have any news, do let me know.

I remain

> your most devoted son
> Hölderlin

GIORGIO AGAMBEN

9 April. Conz writes to Kerner, suggesting he expand the collection with Hölderlin's 'quite good' (*recht brave*) poems published by Stäudlin in 1792–93:

His later ones certainly aren't his best, particularly those from the period when he was beginning to go mad, many of which (halfcrazed) were published in Frankfurt . . . In general . . . collecting these poems is a delicate endeavour. I myself attempted it once, and spoke to Cotta, but he replied with the usual narrowmindedness and *reservatis mentis Cottanae.* Hölderlin's mother and sister had kept many of his papers, and I had selected a fair number— partly demonic stuff, tinged with idealist philosophy and dictated from cloud nine, but also some truly sincere stuff . . . I haven't seen Hölderlin in a year . . . although he used to stop by often. During the summer he frequently came to my garden, uttering a few semisensible words, but then soon got lost again in his usual chatter of half-French, half-German words and highfalutin compliments like 'Your Grace' and 'Your Most Serene Highness', his gaze lost in the far-off sky, his face and mouth making grimaces, as you yourself have seen. He has been much quieter for some time now, but

164

no longer ventures into the courtyard, as he used to enjoy doing. Perhaps I shall visit him this spring.

**Mid-May.** Conz writes to Kerner again, suggesting new poems for inclusion and reporting on his visit with Hölderlin:

> I did visit, speaking first with Zimmer, in his room, and then with Hölderlin, in his cell . . . Hölderlin is now quite calm, but also seems much older than the last time I saw him. Over the course of our entire conversation he said nothing that was complete nonsense, but unfortunately said nothing that made complete sense, either. He unfortunately still insists on all his usual greetings—'Your Grace', 'Excellency', etc. I was only barely able to bring up the subject of his poems and the proposed collection, to which he replied, 'As Your Grace commands.'

It is noteworthy that even a well-meaning friend would consider Hölderlin's poems and philosophical writings to have been written in a state of presumed insanity, even though the only evidence for that would seem to be the overly ceremonious greetings the poet deployed. Hölderlin communicated with Zimmer on a daily basis *without* using ceremonial titles—and Zimmer was the first to hypothesize that the poet, after deciding to suspend communication with almost all other human beings, used this tactic to keep visitors at a distance:

> You may have heard of his habit of giving lofty titles to strangers who visit him. This is his way of keeping people at a distance. Make no mistake, in spite of everything, he is a free man, and you must not step on his toes . . . When he addresses you with such titles, it's his way of saying *leave me alone.*

A month prior—20 April—Gok had written to Kerner to inform him that a small collection of poems had been discovered in Nürtingen. Hölderlin had written them between the ages of 17 and 19, and 'seems to have kept them more as a souvenir for his family than for publication'. At the same time, Gok relays the concern of the poet's mother that any edition of his poems published without due precaution might upset his state of mind, which was apparently 'quite calm at the moment, thank God'. He adds: 'I visited poor Hölderlin the year before, on my way back from Switzerland, and you can imagine what an impression seeing him made on me. He looked good for his age, and was friendly and calm, but I was deeply aggrieved to find his spirit was still so absent that he did not recognize me.'

Here, too, Zimmer's account is informative: 'Hölderlin cannot stand his relatives, and when they come to visit him after so many years he is enraged. I heard that his brother married the woman he was in love with.'

In any case, Gok seems to have hindered rather than facilitated any publication of his brother's poems, first by hinting that a reissue of *Hyperion* might be censored, and then by suggesting that Kerner, as an 'esteemed national poet', should himself oversee Cotta's planned edition.

**14 August.** Cotta writes to Gok and agrees to reissue *Hyperion*, but makes no mention of any other poetry collection. Subsequently—on 22 November, after an exchange of letters—he proposes a fee of 100 Gulden for the reissue of *Hyperion* and 1 Carolin (11 Gulden) for the poetry collection, plus a bonus of one Carolin if 500 copies are sold within four years.

Hölderlin writes to his mother:

My esteemed Mother,
I must always reassure you how grateful I am for your goodness, and how your fine qualities

inspire me to emulate your virtue. Happy are those who know how to encourage virtue and progress in others, for they see how the example they set promotes goodness, which positively influences others' minds. Happiness is happy in and of itself, but it is also thus because of the consideration afforded it, and the hope that it shall be supported by others working for goodness. I trust you will be content with these few words. I remain

your devoted son

Hölderlin

**1 September.** Gok replies to Cotta, proposing that he give Dienst half the fee for the second edition of *Hyperion* and that he give the other half, in Hölderlin's name, to the recently founded Association for the Liberation of Greece, 'my brother's spiritual homeland'. He adds that he could expand on Dienst's planned collection of 43 poems by more than half and makes an additional offer: 'With the support of a national poet, we could ensure that this collection features an adequate preface, outlining the most salient aspects of Hölderlin's life, and hinting as delicately as possible at his unhappy fate.'

**10 October.** Dienst, writing on behalf of himself and Schulze, refuses remuneration: 'Both because we have no intention of such unjustifiable profit, and because we initially began this project in collaboration with Her Royal Highness Princess Wilhelm of Prussia, who in turn would only participate with the sole and purest goal of obtaining Hölderlin's personal support.' He also states that the volume was edited by Kerner, Fouqué, and Schulze, noting that the latter, 'whose name is well established in the fields of philology and aesthetics', wrote the preface.

Over the following two months Gok, Cotta, Kerner, and Dienst exchange a series of letters discussing the proposed fee, which had struck Dienst as unacceptable ('I fail to understand how Cotta, who I hear is usually generous in these matters, could've proposed such terrible terms'). In early December, Gok accepts 100 Gulden for *Hyperion*, and postpones the volume of poetry pending completion of the selection. Then Dienst, writing on behalf of himself and Schulze, unexpectedly suggests that Gok ask Kerner, 'as a fellow countryman and longstanding friend of Hölderlin', to write the preface and be credited as editor of the edition.

**29 December.** Kerner writes to Gok that he cannot, 'as Dienst implies, act as editor, because this would detract from the poems rather than benefit them'. He then suggests Uhland be asked. 'If Uhland refuses, there's no need for an editor; the poems could simply be published under Hölderlin's name, since he is still alive.' He proposes titling the book *Sämtliche Dichtungen von F. Hölderlin* (The Complete Poems of F. Hölderlin).

That same month Kerner's cousin, Bernhard Gottlieb Denzel, writes to him:

> Hölderlin's best poems can be found in the almanacs of the 1790s. Some also appeared in the *Rheinischen Taschenbuch* between 1797 and 1800. The editor of the latter was a clergyman or professor; I no longer recall his full name, but it began with R. After that, Hölderlin ceased writing lyric poetry. After he left Frankfurt, he stayed in Homburg and worked on his Sophocles (although his translation shows signs of his mental disturbance). I've not read anything by him since.

# 1822

**17 January.** Gok asks Cotta to offer 'a somewhat more adequate fee' for the publication of the poems.

**27 January.** Following a positive response from Cotta, Gok proposes a fee of three ducats per page, which Cotta accepts.

**30 January.** Cotta tells Gok a contract is on its way, although it doesn't arrive for another three months. Just days earlier, Uhland had written to Kerner to confirm he would serve as editor: 'I'd be thrilled to see an edition of Hölderlin's poems completed. And, as I've already told Gok, I'd be happy to help. I recently reread "The Archipelago"—what a magnificent poem!'

**18 March.** Gok writes to Kerner to say he has forwarded the manuscript of poems to Uhland, who 'expressed his sincere joy at this collection, which will help bring more attention to Hölderlin's poetic spirit than all the previous, rather scattered publications combined'. Gok confirms that Uhland will compare the manuscript versions with the printed versions and make all necessary corrections, and that he will carry out this onerous task in collaboration with Professor Schwab. Uhland concurs with you that, out of respect for the poor poet, any hint of extraneous intervention should be avoided; these poems should simply be published under Hölderlin's name, and an announcement in the morning paper can inform the public of the new release . . . According to Uhland, dedicating this collection to a member of the House of Hesse-Homburg, which I had proposed to Dienst, is unnecessary; it will suffice that I send a deluxe copy to Her Highness in Hölderlin's name, without a printed dedication.

**18 April.** Karl Ziller writes to Gok from Reutlingen to say he has received a Hölderlin poem from Frau Mäken, which she 'considers a worthy counterpart to Schiller's "The Gods of Greece"'. He transcribes part of the extraordinary poem 'Griechenland', which begins:

*O ihr Stimmen des Geschicks, ihr Wege des Wanderers!*

Oh ye voices of fate, ye paths of the traveller!

Two months later, on 18 June, Ziller follows up with a manuscript fragment of a lost poem, 'Vomers Landgut', in which he notes 'tones of both idyllic poetry and a successful imitation of Greek epics, uniquely reworked by a highly poetic impetus'.

**14 May.** Cotta sends Gok the contract for the proposed edition of Hölderlin's works. For 'the first edition of the complete poems, which shall be published as soon as the manuscript has been completed and edited by Kerner and Schwab', the agreement stipulates a fee of 3 ducats per printed page, plus an additional bonus of 3 ducats if 500 copies are sold within four years.

Hölderlin writes to his mother:

My esteemed Mother,

I am writing to you and shall aim, insofar as I am able, to say nothing that might displease you. Your welfare and the state of your soul are of the utmost importance to me. If you can be satisfied with that, you will be doing me a favour. You already know how much I pray, and I can only hope I do not annoy you. I remain

your devoted son

Hölderlin

**3 July.** Wilhelm Waiblinger visits Hölderlin for the first time. He will eventually write the first biography of Hölderlin, posthumously published in Leipzig in 1831—Waiblinger having died in Rome in 1830, at the age of twenty-six. The following are excerpts from his diary:

> Back in Urach . . . I had received a poem by the brilliant Hölderlin. Uhland and Schwab will soon publish a volume of his work, and I had learned of the poet's terrible fate from Haug's descriptions. Today, Wurm and I visited him. After climbing a narrow stone staircase from the banks of the Neckar, we found ourselves on a narrow street corner, looking at a handsome house just beyond. The sign out front indicated that it was a carpenter's shop, so we knew were in the right place. Climbing the stairs, we were met by an exceptionally pretty girl. I can't say precisely what enchanted me most—whether it was her large, lively eyes, or her resemblance to Philippine, or her delicate, tender neck, or her lovely young bosom, or her harmonious, petite figure. I stared at her as if inebriated while she asked what we wanted. We were spared having to answer her when, through an open door, we glimpsed a man standing in a small, sparse, whitewashed

room shaped like an amphitheatre. He had one hand tucked into his hip-length trousers and began paying us endless compliments. The girl whispered, 'That's him!' The frightening figure threw me into confusion, but I approached and handed him a letter of recommendation from Court Councillor [*Hofrath*] Haug and Senior Finance Councillor [*Oberfinanzrath*] Weisser. Hölderlin set his right hand on a crate attached to the door, leaving his left hand in his trouser pocket; he was draped in a sweat-stained shirt, and his spirited eyes gazed at me with such compassion and desolation that a chill penetrated my bones.

He then addressed me as 'Your Royal Majesty', and the rest of what he said was either partially inarticulate or partially unintelligible, and often mixed with French. I stood before him like a condemned man, my tongue stiff, my eyes dull, with a feeling of terror throughout my entire being. Oh, to see the most brilliant, most spiritual man—human nature at its richest and greatest—reduced to such a miserable state! A mere twenty years prior, this man's spirit had fully expressed its

**10.** Wilhelm Waiblinger, Self-Portrait, drawing, 1825.

thoughts in such an unspeakably magical way, casting everything into a profoundly poetic whirlwind, and now he hadn't a single clear idea, not even of the most insignificant thing—oh, it's enough to make one forsake God! Wurm was as astonished as I, and Hölderlin asked whether he knew Court Councillor Haug. He replied that, in fact, he knew him well. Hölderlin then bowed, and from an incomprehensible sea of sounds the words 'Your Majesty' emerged. Then he spoke in French again, and looked at us in a complimentary manner, stating, 'I cannot—I am not allowed to answer.' We fell silent, and the girl invited us to speak to him while we remained on the threshold. He then murmured, 'Your Royal Majesty, I am considering becoming a Catholic.' Wurm asked whether he was pleased by recent developments in Greece—Hölderlin had once embraced the Greek world with the intense enthusiasm—whereupon the poet complimented him again and, in the midst of a stream of unintelligible words, said, 'Your Royal Majesty, I am not allowed—I cannot answer.' He said only one sensible thing: when Wurm told him the view of the open countryside from his room was most pleasant, he replied, 'Yes, yes, Your Majesty, it's beautiful, just beautiful!' Then he stood in the middle of the room and bowed several times, almost to the floor, without adding anything we could understand except 'Your Royal Majesty', 'Royal Highnesses'. We couldn't stay any longer and hurried to the carpenter's room after a mere five minutes. The pretty, friendly girl and her mother then told us the whole story, since the day he had come to stay with them. He has been insane for about sixteen years and is now fifty years old. Sometimes he comes to his senses, and his screams and bouts of restlessness have decreased, but he is never completely all right. For the last six years he has been pacing up and down his room all day, murmuring to himself, without doing much of anything else. At night he often remains awake and wanders around the house, often going all the way to the main door. He usually goes out for strolls with the carpenter or writes on every piece of paper he gets his hands on, scribbling a bunch of nonsense, although from time to time his scrawling seems to have an inordinately strange significance. He gave me a roll of these papers, on which I read stanzas that were metrically correct but made no sense. I asked whether I might keep one of these papers, and noted how reminiscent the texts were of Pindar, with frequent repetitions. The parts I could understand were invariably about pain, or Oedipus, or Greece. We said our goodbyes, and as we descended the stairs we saw him again through the open door, walking around the room. A shiver of horror ran through me, the scene reminded me of an animal pacing up and down in its cage, and we hurried home in a daze.

I couldn't get this atrocious visit out of my mind for the rest of the day. I incessantly thought about Hölderlin. I couldn't forget the lovely girl, either, and found it sweet to know I would see her again on the next visit. At midday I left for Stuttgart, still daydreaming about Hölderlin and the girl. As I took my leave, she came to meet me on the stairs, holding a jug in her hand.

It is strange indeed that Waiblinger was surprised by the honorifics Hölderlin ascribed to him, when he himself handed over a letter of recommendation from people he addressed using their official titles (court councillor, senior finance councillor). Waiblinger failed to understand that the poet was simply being ironic, extending those ceremonial titles to everyone.

**6 August.** Waiblinger receives a copy of *Hyperion* from Uhland.

> I'm thrilled by Hölderlin. God, oh God! To encounter such thoughts—such a subtle, lofty, and pure spirit—in a madman! I cannot move. *Hyperion* is full of constraint, full of spirit . . . Hölderlin shakes me to the core. I find his work infinitely rich and nourishing. Reading his work allows my entire bosom to open up—I feel a kinship with this great, inebriated soul—oh, Hölderlin—sheer madness.

**9 August.**

> *Hyperion* deserves immortality as much as *Werther* and more than [Friedrich Gottlieb Klopstock's] *The Messiah* . . . Hölderlin is one of the most intoxicated, divinely possessed men. The earth produces few such men, such sacred initiate priests of holy nature . . . I feel terribly compelled to write an epistolary novel . . . I

must write it at once, I must write it now . . .
I need to know more about this madman.

**10 August.** 'My novel's protagonist is a Hölderlin of
sorts, one who goes insane due to divine intoxication,
out of his love of and desire for the divine.'

**11 August.** 'I'm writing a novel! . . . I'm aiming for a
profoundly fantastic tone—not your average Werther—
something special, something absolutely original . . . If
I don't go mad, like my artist, I shall have achieved
something great. Finally, I'll put Hölderlin's story to
good use.'

**1 September.**

> A spirit like Hölderlin—who through some
> frightful disturbance has fallen from celestial
> innocence into the most atrocious contamina-
> tion—amounts to something more than the
> weak beings who remain forever stuck on
> the same track. Hölderlin is my man. His
> life embodies the great, terrible mystery of
> humanity. This lofty spirit had fall, otherwise
> it would not have been so lofty. Consider all
> the poets: Bürger, Matthison [*sic*], Tiedge, Uz,
> Kramer [*sic*], Kleist, Kosegarten, Weisser,

Neuffer, Haug—what are they, compared with him?

**24 October.** 'I visited Hölderlin again. I asked him many questions, and the first words he said were lucid, but the rest were frightful nonsense. As I left to see the carpenter, Hölderlin told the girl that he knew me, that I had been to see him, that I was a kind man. I shall write him.'

In his 1831 biography, Waiblinger reports that one of the phrases Hölderlin repeated most often was: *Es geschieht mir nichts*, literally 'nothing happens to me'. In the life of a poet in a tower, nothing can happen.

**26 November.**

> I spoke with Conz for an entire hour. He told me about Schiller and Hölderlin. Without love there is neither being nor life. Without love there is no spirit, no God, no nature! ... Oh! I shall be, and I shall be happy—happy through love. Misguided projects for the sake of glory, extreme stress, and star-crossed love all drove the great Hölderlin mad. Will it be the same for me?

# 1823

**22 February.** Waiblinger, who has settled in Tübingen and rented a house with a garden in Osterberg, continues to frequent Hölderlin. 'I once again stood, trembling, beside the mad Hölderlin. He played the piano, which I have no doubt he could easily do for eight days straight. He paid me no heed and wasn't disturbed by my presence.'

**23 February.** '*En kai pan*! I'd like to hang this phrase on the wall of my little garden house.'[1]

---

1 F. H. Jacobi had reported the following remark by G. E. Lessing, from a conversation about Goethe's poem *Prometheus*: 'The point of view in which the poem is cast is my own point of view . . . The orthodox concepts of the divinity are no longer for me; I cannot stand them. *Hen kai Pan*! [One and All]. I know naught else.' Gérard Vallée (ed.), *The Spinoza Conversations Between Lessing and Jacobi: Text with Excerpts from Ensuing Controversy* (Lanham, MD: University Press of America, 1988), p. 10. In the 1795 *Vorletzte Fassung* (penultimate version) of *Hyperion*, Hölderlin had written: 'The blessed Unity, Being in the unique sense of the word is lost for us. And we had to lose it if we were to strive, to fight for it. We tear ourselves away from the peaceful *Hen kai Pan* of the world in order to reconstruct it through ourselves.' Hölderlin, *Sämtliche Werke*, VOL. 3 (Stuttgart: Kohlhammer Verlag, 1957), p. 236.

**23 March.** Zimmer writes to Hölderlin's mother that her son's condition has suddenly improved.

Recently, Hölderlin seems to have just woken up from a long sleep. He spends all day with our family, reading the newspaper—he even asked me if Württemberg has become a kingdom. He was surprised when I confirmed it had. He is also interested in the Greeks and read about their victory. I told him that the entire Peloponnese was free of the Turks. 'Amazing,' he cried, 'I'm happy about that!' He talked to my [son] Christian in French, and still speaks it quite well. He told Christian in French that if the weather is good, he'll take more walks around Osterberg. I can't yet return *Hyperion* to you. He reads it every day and also reads Conz's translations of the Greek poets. Sometimes he also borrows some of Christian's copies of the classics and reads them.

**8 June.** Waiblinger records in his diary:

I visited Hölderlin and invited him for a walk tomorrow. He has been in bed for several days, and only walks back and forth along the walls in the morning. He reads his *Hyperion* a lot. One of his quirks is that he sets the dishes outside the door of his room as soon as he has finished eating. He also told me a few crazy things.

**9 June.** Waiblinger continues:

Today Hölderlin, still lying in bed, conjured the most incredible excuses and refused to go out with my royal majesty. The carpenter told me more about his life.

Apparently onanism contributed to his downfall, too, but his life remains infinitely rich. He could have become the number-one German lyric poet. In the mornings these days he paces back and forth, following the wall, until around noon. Young Zimmer finally persuaded him to get up. Hölderlin immediately recognized me and apologized rather absurdly. He constantly repeats, 'Your Majesty, Your Holiness, Your Grace, Your Excellency, Lord Father! Most Gracious Sir, please accept my subservience' [*meine Unterthänigkeit*]. I suggested he come to my Pantheon. The sight of the magnificent spring morning finally seemed to persuade him. I asked him a thousand questions but only received incomprehensible or nonsensical answers in return. When I asked, 'How old are you, Librarian, sir?' he replied, amidst a profusion of words in French, 'I don't know any more, Your Grace.' I tried in vain to remind him of things. Zimmer was astonished that he came to my little house and was incredulous when I told him Hölderlin had smoked a pipe which I filled and lit for him, which he seemed to enjoy. When I invited him to sit at my desk and write a poem he did so, titling the five rhymed lines 'Spring' and handing the work to me with a deep bow. Until that moment, he had talked to himself incessantly, repeating: 'That's right: not now! True! I am truly devoted to Your Grace, and restate my subservience to Your Grace—yes, yes, more than I can say, Your Grace is too kind.' When I told him that I, too, wish to become a poet, and showed him my manuscript, he stared at me and bowed, saying: 'You do! You do? Your Majesty writes? That's right.' When I told him of Haug's misfortune, he shouted 'Oh!' with deep feeling. He asked me how old I was, too. But as soon as he stopped writing, he fell silent, and stared out the window for a long time. Last time he remarked, 'What Your Grace has is extraordinarily beautiful', but didn't say that this time. He just lowered his eyes again, deep in thought, and remained motionless, just barely moving his lips and making a convulsive sound. Then he finally grabbed his hat and left with us, in silence, without saying a word, without paying us any compliments, and without walking just behind us, as he had previously done, as a gesture of courtesy. With a melody on his lips, he then took his leave, paying me a series of clear compliments. I find it difficult to believe he will ever fully return to his senses, his physical weakness alone prevents him from doing so; but it is possible to calm him down, reassure him, pacify him—and I believe I succeeded in doing so, even if only for a few hours. He seems to have a lot of confidence in me, as his behaviour today proved. I'd like to take him to Osterberg more often and try to remain close to him in every way.

**15 June.** 'Hölderlin came to my house and read to me from his *Hyperion*. Oh! I still feel like a child full of joy. Hölderlin is my dearest friend! But he's also crazy. Oh, I could kiss those bare, emaciated lips!'

**9 July.** Waiblinger writes to Friedrich Eser, 'Hölderlin often visits my garden house, and has incredible faith in me. He read my *Phaeton* and made a prophecy: "You

**11.** J. G. Schreiner and R. Lohbauer, *Portrait of Hölderlin*,
drawing, 1823.

shall become a great Lord, Your Holiness!" He's writing poems at my place.'

**27 July.** Mörike visits Hölderlin, accompanied by Rudolf Lohbauer and Gottlob Schreiner, a lithographer, and writes: 'The two of them drew the poor man's profile, almost as a joke, on a piece of paper that I still have.' Waiblinger gives Mörike some papers written by Hölderlin, 'Two metrical poems and some letters that are a continuation of the novel *Hyperion*. They are remarkable and moving because of the enormous contrast with his earlier work. Both poems partially hint at some stupendous significance, and partially display it with clarity. Madness is such an enigma.'

Hölderlin writes to Karl Gok:

Dearest brother,

I trust you will welcome my writing to you. You must know it is a real joy for me to hear you are well and healthy. Even if I write you only briefly and occasionally, please accept this letter as a sign of my attentiveness to you. I must close here, but hope you will keep me in your good thoughts and remain

your admiring brother

Hölderlin

# 1824

**1 July.** Waiblinger writes in his diary: 'Hölderlin plays the piano and sings.'

Hölderlin writes to his mother:

My esteemed Mother,

As you know, I will always gladly write to you, since you are aware of what I have become, and I habitually feel that my way of making myself comprehensible is as it must be. Please always write me letters which require that I reply with all due courtesy. I remain

> your devoted son
> Hölderlin

Emma von Niendorf's book *Reisescenen in Bayern, Tyrol und Schwaben* (Stuttgart, 1840) includes the following passage, presumably about Mörike's visit to Hölderlin: 'During his years at university, Mörike often visited the unhappy poet. The poet often had lucid and beautiful moments, but when he got entangled in a sentence and felt unable to extricate himself, he would conclude with a final, decisive statement, "Z, ja!" (presumably the last letter of the alphabet).'

# 1825

Theodor Vischer, who was a student in Tübingen from 1825 to 1830, writes of having visited Hölderlin four times.

> One could talk to him and, for fleeting moments, understand one another. At times the meaning of his words was perfectly logical, at other times it grew obscure. He suffered from incoherence [*Zusammenhangslosigkeit*], and his thoughts were disjointed, but he had no obsessions . . . His face still bore the traces of a great handsomeness—a high, clear forehead, a proud and noble nose, a well-sculpted chin reminiscent of the ancient Greeks.

**13 May.** Uhland sends Karl Gok the collection of Hölderlin's poems,

> as it will be published, edited by Schwab and myself . . . We decided to omit everything from the period in which his unique poetic excellence had yet to develop, such as the hymns published by Stäudlin, which are obvious imitations of Schiller; everything from his period of mental disturbance has also been excluded.

Deciding where to draw the line with the latter was no easy task, but pieces like 'Patmos' and 'Chiron' could not be included. If Germany still has even the slightest poetic sense left, this collection will cause a stir.

Presumably taking dictation from the poet, Zimmer transcribes two stanzas dedicated to him onto the back of the manuscript page with the poem 'What Is God?':

*Von einem Meschen sag ich, wenn der ist gut*
*Und weise, was bedarf er? Ist irgend eins*
*Das einer Seele gnüget? Ist ein Halm, ist*
*Eine gereifteste Reb' auf Erden*
*Gewachsen, die ihn nähre? Der Sinn is des*
*Also. Ein Freund ist oft die Geliebte, viel*
*Die Kunst. O Teurer, dir sag ich die Wahrheit.*
*Dädalus Geist und des Walds ist deiner.*

About a man, I say, if he be virtuous
And wise, what more can he need? Can anything
Satisfy a soul? Can stalk or stem
Or ripened vine on the earth
Truly nourish? What I mean, then,
is: a friend can be one's beloved, and art
counts for much. My dear man, here's the truth:
Daedalus' spirit, and the forests', is yours.

## 1826

**23 February.** Waiblinger sends Adolf Müllner a poem titled 'To Hölderlin', which begins, '*Komm herauf, / Jammerheiliger / Blick auf / mit deine irren Auge / Deiner Jugendschöne, / Deines Kinderherzens / offnem Nebelgrab*'. ('Arise, / o piteous saint / and gaze / with your wild eyes / upon the uncovered sepulchre / of your youthful beauty, of your childlike heart'.)

In a note accompanying the poem, he writes that the publication of the new edition of *Hyperion* wasn't received as well as it deserved, and 'the purest sparks of poetic talent are nearly as faint in the mad poet's soul as in the eyes of the public'. Waiblinger goes on to announce a forthcoming publication, 'a description of [Hölderlin's] present-day life', which 'will address all the most interesting things that can be said about the battle between titanic aspiration and tragic fate'. He adds:

> As for this poem, it may be useful to know that the mad poet of *Hyperion* spent a whole summer visiting me at my house, where Wieland used to live. It has a garden, and an enchanting view. Apparently, this region reminds

the poor man of his sweetest, saddest, and now most sacred memories. While visiting me, he read *Hyperion* aloud, as well as some poems written in a style that can be frightening.

Hölderlin dedicates a poem to Waiblinger:

> *Wenn Menschen fröhlich sind, wie ist es eine Frage?*
> *Die, ob sie auch gut sei'n, ob sie der Tugend leben;*
> *Dann ist die Seele leicht, und seltner ist die Klage*
> *und Glauben ist demselben zugegeben.*

When people are happy, how can one question
Whether they are good or live by virtue?
For the soul is light, and scarce any lamentation,
And they are granted faith.

Hölderlin pens a series of phrases and mottos for his visitors:

> Herrn von Sillaer:
> *Omnes homines sunt praecipue boni*
> (All men are especially good)

> Herrn von Martizaer:
> *Homines sunt eis praecipue non infensi*
> (Men are especially not enemies)

> Herrn von Sommineer:
> *Quomodo homines sunt, ita est eis participatum*
> (As men are, so is their share)

Herrn von Paristeer:
*Homines sunt tales, quomodo illi praecipue sunt inter se*
(Men are such as they are especially among
themselves)

Herrn von Zirwizaer:
*Homines sunt praecipue tales, quomodo illi sunt inter
se boni*
(Men are especially such, as they are good to one
another)

**Early June.** Cotta finally publishes Hölderlin's poems.
Gok sends a copy to his brother and encloses a letter
apologizing that he couldn't deliver the book in
person:

> Now the fruits of your excellent poetry are
> preserved for the whole world, and through
> them your memory will be honoured by every
> learned and deeply sensitive man . . . The fee
> Cotta paid for the poems and to reissue
> *Hyperion* has been given to your mother in
> Nürtingen; it is your property, and can be used
> as you see fit . . . I hope to be able to visit you
> this summer, if my other obligations allow.
> Perhaps my wife and our two children, Karl
> and Ida, will be able to come, too—they have
> long wanted to see their uncle.

According to one account, Hölderlin was deeply dis-
satisfied by the publication, noting that he 'had no
need of help, and was perfectly capable of publishing
what he himself had written'.

Hölderlin writes to his mother:

Dearest Mother,

I must ask you to assume the burden of taking
in what I had to tell you and thinking about
it. I have had to speak to you with the clarity
you demanded of the task you said you wanted
to assign me. I must tell you that you mustn't
burden yourself with the feelings imposed by
what you know. I remain

your devoted son

Hölderlin

Mörike and Schreiner visit Hölderlin again, and
Schreiner draws a charcoal portrait of the poet, which
Mörike says 'looks a lot like him'.

## 1827

**24 January.** Uhland writes to Varnhagen von Ense complaining he wasn't given the chance to correct the proofs of the collection of Hölderlin's poems. 'We fished the fragments of *Empedocles* from the avalanche of manuscripts . . . We are not responsible for any typos. We had asked for a chance to review everything and make revisions but, after the manuscripts sat on hold for a long while, we were then suddenly presented with almost the entire book, printed in Augsburg. I compiled a long list of errors after reviewing some of the typescript pages, and tried to remedy them as best I could, albeit without comparing them to the original manuscripts.'

**20 March.** Uhland writes to Kerner: 'Did Gok send you a copy of Hölderlin's poems? They've caused a sensation!'

Hölderlin writes to his mother:

My esteemed Mother,
I am free, thanks to the permission of the good Herr Zimmer, to profess my devotion to you and remain,

your most devoted son,

Hölderlin

In the spring, Gustav Schwab publishes an essay on Hölderlin's poetry in *Blätter für literarische Unterhaltung*.

# 1828

In February, Arnim publishes an essay in the *Berliner Conversationsblatt* titled 'Ausflüge mit Hölderlin' (Excursions with Hölderlin), in which he criticizes Uhland and Schwab for omitting some poems from their collection, and includes a prose version of the ode 'Patmos'.

**17 February.** Johanna Christiana Gok dies in Nürtingen and is buried two days later. According to a letter Zimmer wrote to the poet's sister, Hölderlin didn't appear to react: 'Since he received the letter with the mournful news, I have not spoken of you or your dear departed mother, for fear that it might upset him again. Nor has he said anything to me about it.' Schwab's biography reports: 'Her [his mother's] death seems to have made little impression on Hölderlin. His mind was no longer subject to the laws which, at least momentarily, naturally and necessarily govern even the most brutal men.'

**20 February.** The last will and testament are unsealed; Hölderlin is represented by his guardian, Israel Gottfried Burk. A dispute immediately arises between

Karl Gok, his sister Heinrike Breunlin, and Hölderlin's representative regarding the division of the estate's assets: 18,863 Gulden. The royal court in Stuttgart only issues its ruling the following year, on 29 September 1829. Without taking into account his mother's will or the fact that Hölderlin was also entitled to the inheritance from his own biological father and late sister, Gok argues that his half-brother isn't entitled to anything, having already received far too much for his subsistence. The court, considering Christiana Gok's financially secure status and the fact that she benefitted from additional funding to help support her ailing son, awards 5,230 Gulden each to Gok and his sister, and 9,074 Gulden to 'Magister Hölderlin'. According to the ruling, Hölderlin had long since been entitled to make use of his father's inheritance, but had let his mother act as administrator and only received small subsidies in cases of dire need. Two months later, commenting on the inheritance, Zimmer writes to Burk: 'It's sad that he hasn't even been granted what his mother left to him; here, once again, fate hounds him. What will his future biographer—should there be one, as I hope there will—have to say about this story?'

**15 April.** The tailor Philipp Feucht issues an invoice:

For Herr Helderlin, the Librarian:

| | |
|---|---|
| made a waistcoat on 28 February, | 36 Kreuzer |
| repaired two trousers with buttons, | 28 |
| repaired one trouser 15 April, | 16 |

**16 April.** Zimmer writes to Burk, sending a four-month bill of around 52 Gulden for Hölderlin's living expenses. In addition to set costs for room and board, the total, 'from Candlemas to the Feast of Saint George', includes:

| | |
|---|---|
| snuff, | 1.27 Gulden |
| crockery, | 5.30 |
| barber, | 1.30 |
| wine, | 6 |
| laundry, | 2.24 |
| black neckerchief, | 1.52 |
| cobbler, | 1.42 |
| shopkeeper, | 1.18 |
| tailor, | 1.47 |

In the letter, Zimmer adds: 'I don't know whether you ever met the poor, dear poet Hölderlin or took an interest in him. He is truly noteworthy. A recent newspaper called him Germany's finest elegiac poet, and it's such a pity his magnificent mind now languishes in chains. His spirit, too, is so rich, so deep, that it's nearly unequalled among mortals.'

**19 July.** Zimmer writes to Heinrike Breunlin, enclosing a bill for expenses incurred 'between the Feast of Saint George and the Feast of Saint James' totalling 57 Gulden, including 1 Gulden 36 to cover the cost of lighting, 'which had been forgotten in the previous accounting'. He adds:

> Your brother is very well, he rises at dawn and walks around until seven o'clock in the evening, when he has his dinner and then goes to bed. His bodily strength is still good, and he has a strong appetite. His face has aged a little, since he has lost his front teeth, his lips curl inward, and his chin juts out, but he is no longer discontent. His spirit is calm, and his behaviour is pleasant and considerate, although he doesn't take kindly to strangers who disturb him by trying to talk to him or interrupt his routines and habits.

On this same day, the cobbler Gottlieb Esslinger issues an invoice 'for a pair of slippers for Herr Helderle, 1 Gulden 48'.

**25 August.** Emanuel Nast, an old friend from their university days, visits Hölderlin. The poet doesn't recognize him—or, more likely, doesn't wish to speak to him, not least because Nast had been sent by his half-brother, Karl Gok, presumably to discuss family members' inheritance. In a later letter to Heinrike Breunlin, Zimmer describes the meeting as follows: 'An old university friend, Nast, visited, but Hölderlin didn't acknowledge him. Hölderlin was playing the piano, and Nast cried like a child—overwhelmed with love and sadness, he hugged Hölderlin, exclaiming "dear Hölderle, don't you recognize me?" but Hölderlin just happily kept playing his harmonies and merely nodded his head at the question.'

Rosine Stäudlin, whom Zimmer describes as 'aged, but with lively, brilliant eyes', also pays Hölderlin a summertime visit.

**29 November.** Zimmer writes to Burk, 'I have received the payment you sent for Herr Hölderlin's account, as well as the 100 Gulden you so generously sent ... He [Hölderlin] is not unhappy, has an incredible imagination, and always keeps himself occupied.'

# Gedichte

von

Friedrich Hoelderlin.

---

Und wie du das Herz
Der Pflanzen erfreuest,
Wenn sie entgegen dir
Die zarten Arme strecken,
So hast du mein Herz erfreut,
Vater Helios! und wie Endymion,
War ich dein Liebling,
Heilige Luna!

Fragment.

---

Stuttgart und Tübingen
in der J. G. Cotta'schen Buchhandlung.
1 8 2 6.

**12.** Cover of the poetry collection published in 1826.

# 1829

**10 March–2 June.** A series of opinions (including Uhland's) and official evaluations result in an allowance for the 'mentally ill [*gemüthskranken*] Magister Hölderlin' being granted for his subsistence.

**15 April.** Zimmer writes to Heinrike Breunlin: 'Hölderlin is often very cheerful. When someone in our household plays a waltz, he immediately starts dancing and is often witty. He has been particularly calm this spring, and now his golden age is back, as it's once again the season when he rises at three o'clock in the morning and walking is a true joy for him.'

**18 July.** Zimmer writes to Heinrike Breunlin again:

Your dear brother is well. This summer he hasn't been rising as early as usual, though, getting up instead around five o'clock in the morning, and going to bed at half past eight . . . in the afternoon, when he has his coffee, he doesn't sit, but walks back and forth all day. When he drinks wine, he wanders around as well. On cold days he paces around the house, otherwise he usually goes outside. He's now about sixty years old, but is still a strong man, living peaceably and contented. He seldom shows any discontent—only when he conducts heated debates with imaginary intellectuals in his head.

On this same day Esslinger, the cobbler, issues another invoice.

| | |
|---|---|
| One winter shoe resoled | |
| and the forefoot of another repaired on | |
| 19 September 1828, | 50 |
| One shoe resewn and patched on | |
| 27 January 1829, | 54 |
| and another on 31 January, | 46 |
| Total: | 2 Gulden 30 |

**August.** Neuffer prepares a selection of Hölderlin's odes that were omitted from Uhland and Schwab's collection for publication in the *Zeitung für die Elegante Welt*.

# 1830

**30 January.** Zimmer writes to Heinrike Breunlin, enclosing the usual invoice and adding:

> Your brother is very well. He has already tried to go outside twice but came back in both times due to the cold. One Mr Lebret is rooming with us and has taken a keen interest in your brother. Lebret told me that your brother was in love with his father's sister, and is infinitely saddened by his current sorry state, especially since he used to have such an exceptional mind. Otherwise, there are now many things soothing your brother—his love of music, his sensitivity to nature's beauty, and the visual arts.

During this period, Hölderlin writes two poems for the aforementioned Johann Paul Friedrich Lebret, a law student who was also the nephew of Elise Lebret. According to an annotation on the back of Johannes Mährlen's manuscript sheet, they were written in exchange for a pipeful of tobacco. The first, 'Aussicht' (The View), begins '*Wenn Menschen frölich sind, ist dieses vom Gemüte*' (When men are happy, it comes from the soul); the second, 'Dem gnädigsten Herrn von Le

Bret', begins, '*Sie, Edler! sind der Mensch, von dem das Beste sagen*' (You, noble sir, are the man all speak so highly of).

**6 March.** Princess Maria Anna of Prussia writes in her diary:

> Yesterday the current *Rector magnificus*, the world-famous professor Hegel, came to see us. It was most embarrassing for me, I was nearly too ashamed to speak with him, I felt confused and didn't know what to say. Then Mr Sinclair, whom Hegel had known for a long time, came to mind, so I began to talk about him ... then Hegel started talking about Hölderlin, who is lost to the world, and about his book *Hyperion* which, thanks to my sister Auguste, had made quite an impression on me when I was young. I felt a deep joy hearing that name, it opened the door to an entire past era, and at that moment Hölderlin was so dear to me, like an echo. A kind of memory was awakened, in a way usually sparked by a sound or melody. At the same time, I saw in my mind's eye the book *Hyperion* again, with its green binding, perched on my sister Auguste's window before a beautiful backdrop of vines and sunlight outside,

with cool shadows along the avenue of brown chestnut trees, and I heard the birds—suddenly a moment from the past was revealed to me solely through the sound of that friendly name.

According to a letter Zimmer wrote in 1835 ('A few years ago he composed these lines about himself . . . '), this was likely also the period when Hölderlin wrote this poem:

*Nicht alle Tage nennet die schönsten der,*
*Der sich zurücksehnt unter die Freuden, wo*
*Ihn Freunde liebten, wo die Menschen*
*über dem Jüngling mit Gunst verweilten.*

Not every day will be deemed the happiest
By he who yearns for pleasurable times past
When he was loved by friends, and when
People showed his young self such favour.

**8 March.** Zimmer and Hölderlin's guardian sign an agreement stipulating that an annual lump sum of 250 Gulden be paid to support Hölderlin ('146 for room and board, 24 for wine, 8 for afternoon coffee, 6 for snuff and the same amount for the barber . . . ').

# 1831

*Zeitgenosse*, a magazine based in Leipzig, posthumously publishes Waiblinger's biographical essay 'Friedrich Hölderlins Leben, Dichtung und Wahnsinn' (Friedrich Hölderlin's Life, Poetry and Madness). Waiblinger had left Tübingen in 1826 and moved to Rome, where he died on 17 January 1830 (there is now a commemorative plaque on his former home in Via del Mascherone, near Piazza Farnese, which reads *Qui solamente felice*, 'Only happy here'). One passage from Waiblinger's essay reads:

> What can occupy him for a whole day is his *Hyperion*. Hundreds of times, when I paid him a visit, I heard him declaiming from it in a loud voice. His pathos was impressive, and *Hyperion* almost always was there lying at hand. Often, he would read me passages. When he had finished a particular part, he would exclaim with ponderous gesticulations: 'Wonderful, wonderful, Your Majesty!' He began reading again and then suddenly sat down, saying: 'You see gracious sir, a comma!' He also read aloud the books I had offered to him. But he understood

nothing of them because he was too distracted, he could never even follow one of his own thoughts, still less that of someone else ... The only other books [he reads] are the *Odes* of Klopstock, those of Gleim, Cronegk and other older poets of this stable. He often reads the *Odes* and quotes from them. I told him innumerable times that his *Hyperion* would be reprinted, and that Uhland and Schwab were in the midst of collating his poems. But I received no response other than a deep bow and the words: 'You are a good soul, Herr Waiblinger! I am obliged to you, Your Holiness.'

**22 April.** Zimmer issues a receipt: '62 Gulden received from Mr Burk, guardian, for the four-month period from Candlemas to the feast of Saint George, to cover Magister Hölderlin's expenses.'

# 1832

**21 January.** Zimmer writes to Burk:

I am pleased to report that your ward is doing very well. He is generally docile and courteous, and spends his winter days playing the piano, which amuses him greatly. He also sings as he plays, although his voice isn't as pleasant now as it was last spring. When he isn't seated at the piano he moves about incessantly all day, and only in the evening does he sit for a while at dinner.

Mörike writes to Johannes Mährlen:

I have read *Hyperion* again. When I reread it, I was troubled, despite all its magnificence, by an inescapable feeling of wrongness, as if the entire subject and structure were misguided. Sometimes even the description of the main character struck me that way; the protagonist is purely elegiac (or so Hölderlin himself claims), and yet he is saddled with rather uneven, grand aspirations. In the end, the whole thing seems a bit like a caricature—albeit a moving one— with some truly genuine lines of unparalleled beauty somewhat agonizingly applied to the plot. The reader comes away with an impression that is distressing yet joyous. One feels rapt, as if the hand of a god had suddenly plucked the most delicate string of one's soul. It is powerfully uplifting, but then one plummets again, and is left feeling so ill, so pusillanimous, so miserable, that every trace of poetry, even of *tragic* poetry, is lost.

**18 June.** Prior to this date, Hölderlin writes his first rhymed poem, titled 'Der Frühling' ('Spring'), which begins:

*Wie selig ist, zu sehen, wenn Stunden wieder tagen*
*Wo sich vergnügt der Mensch umsieht in den Gefilden,*
*Wenn Menschen sich um das Befinden fragen,*
*Wenn Menschen sich zum frohen Leben bilden . . .*

How blissful it is to watch the hours dawning
As people contentedly contemplate the fields,
When they reflect on how things are going,
When they work towards life's serene yield . . .

**21 June.** Zimmer issues an invoice: 'My wife bought a jacket for Hölderlin . . . 1 Gulden 28.'

**1 December.** The Württemberg Ministry of the Interior issues a report on the state of the mentally ill in the city of Tübingen.

Name: Magister Hölderlin

Age: 62 years

Religion: Protestant

Profession and marital status: librarian, single

Duration of illness: 29 years

Nature of mental illness: confused (*verwirrt*)

Support: from the family

Notes: meek

Causes of illness: unrequited love, exhaustion, over-zealous studies

## 1833

**29 January.** Zimmer writes to Burk:

Enclosed please find the receipt for your payment covering the last quarter. I should especially like to thank you for the generous donation of 22 Gulden, which greatly surprised us. Hölderlin will always be treated according to your good wishes. He is doing well, is serene, and sleeps quite well, often singing and playing [piano] for half the day.

**18 April.** Zimmer writes to Burk:

Hölderlin is faring very well . . . two days ago a gentleman came to us at eight o'clock in the evening with a head of lettuce atop his own head. He wanted to enter Hölderlin's room, implying that he was from Nürtingen and was following orders from Hölderlin's sister. Since Hölderlin was already in bed, we turned him away. He promised to come back the next day, but then didn't. On his way out he proceeded to declaim from Hölderlin's *Hyperion*, and it was clear he wasn't in his right mind . . . I am enclosing cobbler Müller's latest bill, dated 15 April.

Herr Helderle:

| | |
|---|---|
| 16 February, repaired a shoe, | 52 |
| 8 March, completely resoled a shoe, | 48 |
| total | 1.40 Gulden |

**6 November.** Zimmer writes to Burk:

Your ward absolutely needs a new pair of trousers, for which I enclose a bill for the fabric, from seamstress Friederike Maier; the tailor hasn't yet made the trousers, otherwise I'd include his bill, too. Hölderlin is doing well and quite happy. He keeps busy reciting Klopstock's odes, reading from Homer, and singing with great passion.

For Herr Magister Hölderlin:

| | |
|---|---|
| two pairs of knitted wool socks, | 16 Kreuzer |
| wool, | 30 |
| darned several pairs of stockings, | 24 |
| total | 1.10 Gulden |

## 1834

**23 May.** An announcement is published in the *Stuttgarter Beobachter:*

> Back in 1828, in his 'Excursions with Hölderlin' in the *Berliner Conversationsblatt*, Achim von Arnim brought attention to the fact that poems had been omitted from the collection published by Cotta. These unpublished poems should no longer be withheld from the public, which is interested in Hölderlin's poetic gifts and tragic fate. We therefore believe that we speak on behalf of a large number of avid readers of literature when we earnestly request that anyone in possession of the aforementioned poems urgently respond to this call.— Many admirers of Hölderlin's muse.

**May or June.** Uhland, who rightly reads this announcement as a criticism of Gok, Schwab, and himself, prepares a response. After pointing out that Arnim's note referred not to unpublished poems, but rather to poems that had already appeared in Seckendorf's *Musenalmanach* of 1807 and 1808, he adds:

Our intention was that the first collection of this excellent poet's work highlight his most mature, strongest qualities. We left out that which, once he had duly obtained broader recognition, would only be of interest insofar as it contributes to an understanding of his personal biography. Those who go to the trouble of carefully inspecting the manuscripts we worked from, which were obtained from Hölderlin's relatives, will be convinced that we successfully preserve, at least in fragments, even the works that were most difficult to decipher, such as *Empedocles* . . . Therefore, we can only hope that these hitherto unnamed 'admirers of Hölderlin's muse' will now come forward, naming not only themselves but also those who, being in possession of unpublished poems by Hölderlin, they feel obliged to accuse of having kept such works hidden.

**18 July.** Zimmer writes to Burk:

In sending you this bill, I can also send you good news about your ward. His life is absolutely regular. He gets up at three o'clock in the morning and walks around until seven o'clock, when he has breakfast. Then he often plays the piano and sings for two hours straight, and the remaining hours of the day he walks to and fro. In the evening he retires to his room and passionately recites the work of various poets. At night he sleeps quite peacefully, even on the coldest nights. His appetite and health are very good.

One proof of how much he loves music is that when the two gentlemen who live below him play, he immediately opens the window and listens in. His character is also good, he is well behaved, and just doesn't want to be ordered around.

**Autumn.** Adolf Friedrich von Schack mentions a visit to Tübingen in a text subsequently published as *Erinnerungen und Aufzeichnungen* ('Recollections and Observations', Stuttgart and Leipzig, 1888):

I was driven to Tübingen by a desire to see Friedrich Hölderlin. I knew I would see little more than a wreck, since the poet had fallen into an incurable madness nearly thirty years prior. But, even in the face of this wreck, I found myself as moved as one would when deep in meditation before a Greek temple ... One must read the work of Heinrich von Kleist, [Johann

Gottfried] Seume, and Hölderlin. It may be surprising to see me list Seume beside the other two, for his poetic talents certainly do not equal theirs. Hölderlin was seized, even before Kleist, by the same fate that will likely befall many other poets of our country. As I stood in front of the window of the room in which Hölderlin used to dwell, the terrible and crushing words he levelled against the Germans in his *Hyperion* came to mind ... Hölderlin's misfortune strikes my anguished soul as even more terrible than Kleist's.

**19 December.** Pfisterer, the tailor, issues an invoice:

| | |
|---|---|
| Made a dressing gown, | 1.12 |
| threads for the seams, | 8 |
| pockets and belt, | 10 |
| 12 yds calico, | 2.48 |
| 9 yds flannel, | 5.60 |
| total | 9.24 |

# 1835

**25 January.** Maier, the seamstress, issues an invoice:

| | |
|---|---|
| 2 pairs of knitted socks, | 24 Kreuzer |
| yarn, | 46 |
| suspenders for trousers, | 30 |
| total | 1.40 |

**22 December.** Zimmer writes to an unidentified person (possibly Adolf von Schack):

Poor Hölderlin was doomed from the very start. While his mother was pregnant with him, she vowed that if he were born a boy, she would ensure his life would be devoted to the Lord, as she put it—in other words, she'd see to it that he became a theologian. When the time came for him to go to a seminary, Hölderlin tried to resist—he wanted to become a doctor—but his ultra-religious mother forced him into it and so, quite against his will, he became a theologian. When he finished his studies, Chancellor Lebret planned to welcome Hölderlin as a parish priest in Wolfenhausen and have him marry his daughter, but Hölderlin refused: first, because he did not want his professional appointment to be contingent upon his taking a wife; second, because he'd never been inclined towards theology, and would never have been able to become an expert in it, whereas he quite enjoyed natural philosophy. Later, Hölderlin went to Frankfurt and became a tutor in the house of a wealthy merchant named Gontard, where he became very close to the lady of the house. This resulted in a disagreement, whereupon Hölderlin left, withdrawing to Homburg. He then planned to become a professor of philosophy in Jena, which did not come to pass. He then returned home, rather melancholic . . . Hölderlin was and still is a great admirer of nature, and he has a broad view overlooking the entire Neckar and Steinlach valleys from his room . . . He has been in my house for 30 years now. I no longer have any difficulty with him, although in the past he often grew infuriated; blood would rush to his head, he'd become red as a brick, and took offence at everything. But as soon as his fit of rage passed, he was the first to extend his hand in a gesture of reconciliation. Hölderlin has a noble heart, is capable of deep emotion, and has a very healthy body. For as long as he has been in my home, he has never fallen ill.

He is handsome and cuts a fine figure—never have I seen such beautiful eyes in the face of a mere mortal.

He is now 65 years old but is as bright and lively as if he were 30. He wrote the following poem in 12 minutes. I asked him to write something for me, too, and he opened the window, gazed out, and in 12 minutes the poem was done ... Hölderlin entertains himself playing the piano, and sometimes also declaiming or even drawing. There is no doubt that he is aware of his state. A few years ago he composed these lines about himself. [The poem that begins 'Nicht alle Tage' follows; see the entry for 1830.]

Since his mother's death, Hölderlin's guardian has been a man named Burk in Nürtingen. He is a good man, and pays me 250 Gulden annually for lodging, wine, laundry and food. The municipal government pays Hölderlin's guardian 150 Gulden annually, for life. Hence, Hölderlin costs him 100 Gulden per year, although I believe Hölderlin has enough means that he doesn't need the additional financial assistance. He enjoys smoking tobacco, too, but I leave that out of the accounting.

## 1836

**9 January.** Heinrike Breunlin tallies up an expense sheet:

For my brother Hölderlin:

Two and a half measures of hemp fabric

| | |
|---|---|
| for a pillow, | 1 Gulden |
| Shipping to Tübingen, | 6 Kreuzer |
| Total, | 1.6 |

**24 January.** Zimmer writes to Burk: 'Most honourable Herr Guardian, enclosed please find the latest four-month statement for your ward, who is doing very well and is also pleasantly behaved towards all . . .'

**July.** Zimmer writes to Burk: 'Your ward is doing very well. Even on the coldest days he is all right, and often dozes off on the sofa. He used to nap only seldom, but he continues to wander around the house in the middle of the night . . . N.B. Hölderlin read this letter and shook his head.'

**3 November.** Müller, the cobbler, issues an invoice:

Note for Herr Hölterle [*sic*]:

28 May, fully resoled a shoe,          50

3 November, a new pair of shoes,      1.36

**5 November.** Zimmer writes to Burk, 'Regarding your ward, everything remains steady. As before, he is doing very well; he was recently visited by Herr Secretary Günther von Esslingen, and played the piano, which he often does for half the day.'

**13.** Hölderlin family coat of arms (with a branch of elder, *Holder* in German).

# 1837

From a note by Gustav Schlesier: 'He [Hölderlin] now signs his work as Scartanelli [*sic*], and calls himself the same. He got it into his head that his name was no longer Hölderlin, but Scartanelli or even Buarooti [*sic*].'

**January.** Zimmer writes to Burk: 'Last night a fire broke out near my home, and there was great commotion in the house, but Hölderlin remained calmly in bed.'

**7 April.** Hölderlin writes to Carl Künzel:

When people ask themselves what good consists of, the answer is that human beings must grant virtue its due honour, and practise in life all that humans strive for. Life is not the same as virtue, because virtue concerns humans directly, whereas life is more distant from humans. Good also generally consists of human beings' interiority. I send you, kind gentleman, my regards.

most devotedly yours,

Buonarotti

**17 April.** Zimmer writes to Burk:

> Fourteen days ago a gentleman came from Dresden for Hölderlin, to pay him a visit. At first Hölderlin was rather curt with him, but soon grew kinder when he realized the man was a scholar and proceeded to calmly converse with him. The visitor handed him a piece of paper and Hölderlin wrote a verse on it, signing his name, which gave him great pleasure.

**July.** Zimmer writes to Burk: 'Your ward is doing very well, and a few days ago he wrote a philosophical poem for one Frau Zimmer who was visiting us.'

**16 September.** Hölderlin writes a poem:

*Der Herbst*

*Die Sagen, die der Erde sich entfernen,*
*Vom Geiste, der gewesen ist und wiederkehret,*
*Sie kehren zu der Menschheit sich, und vieles lernen*
*Wir aus der Zeit, die eilends sich verzehret.*
*Die Bilder der Vergangenheit sind nicht verlassen*
*Von der Natur als wie die Tag' verblassen*
*im hohen Sommer, kehrt der Herbst zur Erde nieder,*
*Der Geist der Schauer findet sich am Himmel wieder.*
*In kurzer Zeit hat vieles sich geendet,*

*Der Landmann, der am Pfluge sich gezeiget,*
*Er siehet, wie das Jahr sich frohem Ende neiget,*
*In solchen Bildern ist des Menschen Tag vollendet.*
*Der Erde Rund mit Felsen ausgezieret*
*Ist wie die Wolke nicht, die Abends sich verlieret,*
*Es zeiget sich mit einem goldnen Tage,*
*Und die Vollkommenheit ist ohne Klage.*

## Autumn

The legends that depart from earth so vast,
And from the spirit which was and shall return,
They turn towards humanity, and much we learn
From time, which consumes itself so fast.
The images of the past are never mislaid
By Nature; the days of summer do fade,
And autumn descends to earth yet again;
A stormy spirit gathers in the heavens.
So much has ended, time is so fleet,
The peasant noted from his plough,
See how the year comes to a glad end now;
Such images make a person's day complete.
The round earth with rock adorned
Is unlike the clouds, which after dusk are scorned;
It reveals itself in the golden day,
And perfection holds all complaint at bay.

Towards the end of the year, the Catholic theologian Albert Diefenbach visits Hölderlin:

A trifling matter led me to carpenter Zimmer's house on the Neckar. A tall, curved, other-worldly figure met me at the door. I was over-come with dismay. The confused stare of his hollow eyes, the convulsive twitching of his facial muscles, the shaking of his grey curls— everything about him evinced the oddness of a madman. An incomprehensible, polyglot flourish of titles ensued—from which I could only make out 'Your Majesty, Your Highness, Your Holiness, Your Grace, Lord Father, kind sir'—followed by a dozen deep bows and other grand gestures of politeness, whereupon he directed me to Zimmer. The first question I asked was who that disturbing person was, and I was astonished by the answer: Hölderlin! . . . His landlord, an educated and friendly man, had the goodness to take me to the old poet's room, under the pretext of showing me the exquisite view from the window, overlooking the Neckar and Steinlach valleys. The mad poet received me with the same ceremony as before, intent as he was on his gesticulations and impassioned declamations. I still feel the

draw of his tall, slightly curved figure, the handsome face of the old man in his seventies, his
stately profile, his high, thoughtful forehead,
and above all his eyes. I've never since seen their
like—they veritably smiled with friendliness yet
were also confused and wild; they were undeniably a bit spent, but still amiable and animated.
Their expression was strengthened further still
by the pained, oppressive, furrowed brow that
hung above them. Hölderlin's once-noble features show the unmistakable, devastating traces
of mental illness, especially in his mouth and
cheeks. Involuntary convulsions course through
his face, shoulders and hands. He wants to be
gentle and friendly with visitors but gets confused: one cannot understand him. His questions and answers are both quick and jumbled,
and he dismisses visitors using the same compliments with which he welcomed them. With
few exceptions, he no longer recognises his
former acquaintances, sometimes not even his
half-brother.

The place he loves most is open nature,
which for him is limited to a small garden
along the Neckar. He often lingers there, by
day and by night, plucking blades of grass and

flowers and tossing them into the river. He dis-
plays a most fervent adoration of children, but
the disturbing old man scares them—they run
away, and then he cries. Back when he could
still contain his madness, he once saved a child
from danger, risking his own life. At the first
rays of dawn, he leaves his bed and wanders the
corridors and little garden of the house for half
the day. The only works he reads are books by
poets he has found in his current home (Us
[*sic*], Zachariae, Cramer, Gleim, Cronegk and
Klopstock) and especially *Hyperion* (in the old
edition). He cannot stand the work of the
newer poets. Despite his brilliant work on
Sophocles, he knows hardly any Greek. He
recites passages from his *Hyperion* or Klopstock,
aloud, for hours on end, with great enthusiasm.
Whenever he comes across a sheet of paper, he
fills it with verses, most of which strictly follow
ancient metre. They are formally correct but
conceptually confused. The only thing he really
succeeds at is describing nature, especially when
he can see what he wants to sing the praises of.
Proof of this is the enclosed manuscript, signed
by Hölderlin, which he wrote on the morning
of my visit [the poem 'Der Sommer', which

begins *Das Erndtefeld erscheint, auf Höhen schim-
mert*] . . . He remembers quite fondly his friend-
ships with Matthisson, Schiller, Zollikofer,
Lavater et al., and all those who loved him. He
doesn't want to hear about Goethe [*will er nicht
kennen*] (Schiller and Eichhorn had proposed
Hölderlin for the endowed professorship in
philosophy at Jena, but Goethe recommended
Niethammer, who ultimately got the job) . . .
He often notices the little things and faithfully
memorizes their every detail. He loves music:
he sits for hours at his landlord's piano and plays
the same musical pieces until he grows tired—
usually simple, childish pieces he remembers
from his happy youth. In the end, the poor
man succumbs to a mad melancholy, closes his
tear-drenched eyes and, raising his head, sings
with great pathos. One cannot understand
what he is saying, but the plaintive sounds are
an expression of profound sadness and make a
powerful impression on the soul of the listener.
Hölderlin was once a superb musician and
vocalist. The students who live in the same
house as him . . . treat him with great affection,
and often invite him for coffee or a glass of
wine.

According to a subsequent account by Christoph Theodor (C. T.) Schwab, Gustav Schwab's son, the music Hölderlin played and sang included the aria 'Mich fliehen alle Freuden' from *Die schöne Müllerin*, the German version of Giovanni Paisiello's opera *L'amore contrastato o la bella molinara*.

Early in the year, Maier, the seamstress, issues an invoice:

For Herr Hölderlin:

| | |
|---|---|
| Mended four shirts, | 26 |
| Mended a dressing gown, | 12 |
| Darned stockings, | 12 |
| Purchased half a pound of thread, | 40 |
| Knitted six pairs of stockings, | 36 |
| Total, | 2.36 Gulden |

**16 April.** Kurz responds to the portrait of Hölderlin that Mörike had sent: 'I saw Hölderlin in Tübingen, and would not have recognized him in this drawing, but when I showed it to Silcher today, he immediately said his name. His lips, I can say with certainty, are both thinner and more pursed; perhaps he has changed over the past ten years. In any case, in its sparse and speedy strokes, this portrayal is quite meaningful.'

**17 April.** Zimmer writes to Burk: 'Your ward is doing very well, as are we. Towards the end of the holidays, he received several visitors, which must have been a burden on him because he ran off, and just left them standing there.'

**26 June.** Mörike writes to Kurz: 'I recently received a pile of Hölderlin's papers, mostly illegible, extremely weak work. But I must share with you a curious religious fragment at least.'

Mörike quotes a few lines, in which the children's catechism is compared to 'sleepy, idle conversation'.

> What do you think of that description? The parts about the catechism sound devilishly naive, however moving they may strive to be. They are followed by an ode to his landlord (I have it here, before my own eyes, in a copy made by the subject himself, who must have felt flattered indeed). The last verse, which refers to carpentry and the forest, is particularly remarkable. [The poem 'To Zimmer' follows, see the entry for 1825.]

Later that summer, Kurz replies to Mörike:

> I find Hölderlin's works highly edifying, precisely because I discovered therein something I've long been unable to articulate but instinctively sought. Indeed, in Hölderlin, I detect an affinity with none other than Hegel. They share a few characteristic impromptus: the former's rendering of the catechism could have been delivered from the lectern by the latter in his

trademark surly tone, his phenomenology teems with similar ideas, and therein lies its value (if one interprets it correctly). But what I didn't dare admit to myself for a long time was that it is precisely through such details (including the passage you sent me) that Hölderlin has always made such a winning impression on me ... Hegel's ideas contain a Germanic tinge, but Hölderlin's prophecies, too, are little more than deepened Swabianisms.

**July.** Zimmer writes to Burk:

Your ward is doing very well, and now has new windows and Venetian blinds in his room, which he scrupulously steered clear of at first. When something pops into his mind at night, he has long had a habit of getting out of bed, opening the window, and articulating his thoughts to the open air. But now, with these new windows, when he tries to open them, he finds them less comfortable, so is not as quick to open them as he used to be.

**Autumn.** Gustav Kühne visits Hölderlin:

No sooner was I on the threshold of the house in which he was staying than a ghastly fear seized me. I saw the surroundings, I saw the window from which the poor poet contemplated the Neckar, the small space in front of the house where he walked every day since he was no longer allowed to roam any farther. Seeing him in person struck me as superfluous, it's rather sad to observe the ruins of former greatness in a dethroned prince . . . At this point my friend, the dear M., entered the room, shaking hands with a stranger and saying, 'This is Hölderlin's host.' The day prior, I had expressed a desire to meet the good carpenter who had been the unfortunate man's guardian, tutor, and friend for thirty years . . .

At this point, Kühne transcribes everything Zimmer says—at length, and as he pronounces it in his Swabian dialect, albeit without adding any information not previously revealed elsewhere. He then goes on to describe meeting the poet:

'There he is!' said the carpenter, 'Come. But don't expect him to play music, he's in a bad mood today. He says the fountain of wisdom has been poisoned, and the fruits of knowledge are like empty purses, pure deceit. See him? He was sitting under the plum tree, gathering the shrivelled fruit. There is often quite a lot of sense in his otherwise confused talk . . . '. The unhappy man now stood on the threshold before us. The carpenter introduced me as a luthier, who had come to tune the spinet. 'No need,' said Hölderlin, 'no need! The tuning requires another kind of repair. It's fine, just fine as is. I have known you for a long time, your dignified reputation precedes you, My Lord. And if it just so happens that everything has gone wrong for me today, Juppiter [*sic*] will hold court and will have no regard even for your sister. *Oui!*' He abruptly fell silent and just stood before us, silent and calm. All across his face, the silence of a battlefield reigned . . . I couldn't bear the sight of it any longer. As we took our leave, the poet bowed deeply and whispered his ceremonious phrases. 'Adieu, dear Hölderlin!' said M. 'Dear Baron von M., I am honoured to salute you and bid you farewell!' was his reply.

**18 November.** Ernst Zimmer dies suddenly, at the age of 86. There are no records of how Hölderlin responded. Going forward, Zimmer's daughter Lotte, who had always had a particularly friendly rapport with the poet, took care of him and all correspondence with his relatives and Burk. Hölderlin called her 'Most Holy Virgin Lotte'.

## 1839

**4 February.** Lotte Zimmer writes to Burk, enclosing the four-month expense record:

Herr Librarian is now rather restless, the thunderstorms have an enormous effect on him, and his demeanour changes every day. He is often quite quiet and calm, or else so restless it's no surprise his mood swings so extremely. At night he often gets up and walks, and we're glad that he has his shirt, which seems to help him a lot, such that he doesn't take it off.'

**20 April.** Lotte writes to Burk again:

Hölderlin is now doing very well, he has only been restless a few days recently, as usual due to changes in the weather, which affects him a lot. Over the holiday we cleaned and repainted his room, so we had to put him up in one of the vacant student rooms, where he stayed for 10 days until everything was done. He particularly enjoyed it because that room had a piano, so he played for hours on end. Each day he came up to see his room, asking when it would be ready, so when he was finally able to return he was thrilled. He was satisfied to see his room had become so beautiful, and thanked us very much.

**24 April** (if the manuscript date is to be trusted). Hölderlin composes the poem 'Der Frühling', which begins, *Die Sonne glänzt, es blühen die Gefilde* ... which, like almost all his poems from 1837 onwards, he signs under the name Scardanelli (or, less frequently, under the name Buonarotti, likely a misspelt reference to Filippo Buonarroti, a revolutionary who was born in Pisa in 1761, died in Paris in 1837, was one of the most radical proponents of communal ownership and egalitarianism, and was also a staunch critic of industrialism).

**12 July.** Louise Gfrörer, seamstress, issues an invoice:

Knitted, per an order from Frau Zimmer:

| | |
|---|---|
| six pairs of socks, | 1 Gulden |
| yarn, | 1 |
| mended one stocking, | 15 Kreuzer |
| total, | 2.15 |

**29 July.** Ludwig Neuffer, one of Hölderlin's close friends from their years in Tübingen and Jena, dies.

**14.** Detail of a poem signed 'Scardanelli' (1841?).

**15 October.** Lotte Zimmer writes to Burk:
We've encountered some difficulty with Herr
Hölderlin, due to his shirts. The new ones they
sent about a year ago are so worn out that they
cannot be mended, and for three others we
had to have new sleeves and collars made . . .
you cannot imagine, his shirts wear out so
much faster than those of men who do heavy
manual labour, because he always has his hands
in his sleeves, and plays [the piano] like that.

**19 December.** Hoffmann, the tailor, issues an invoice:

| | |
|---|---|
| For six shirts, 36 Kreuzer each, | 3.36 |
| thread, | 12 |
| hems, | 10 |
| buttons, | 9 |

**December.** Bettina von Arnim sends Hölderlin's
poems to her young friend Julius Döring for
Christmas, writing: 'This should be every young man's
most cherished book.'

Georg Herwegh writes an essay titled 'Hölderlin—
Ein Verschollener' (Holderlin—A Forgotten Man),
which asserts:

Hölderlin is the authentic poet of youth, and
Germany bears guilt, because Germany allowed

him to fall from grace. Having seen our miserable condition, even before our dishonour brought us to our nadir, he saved himself by plunging into the sacred night-time of madness—he, who had been called to venture on ahead of us, and sing for us a battle song ... As Börne once said, 'That which youth believes is eternal', and this phrase holds true in Hölderlin ... For young people interested in antiquity, he is a much more valuable resource than even the greatest philologist ... Hölderlin knew how big the world was, and simply could not accept how small it had become.

**January** (perhaps). Hölderlin inscribes an unidentified visitor's guest book:

> On the reality of life
> When people realize that knowledge, in life, lies in that which is of interest to them, then it can be said that there is purpose in life, and that usefulness, in life, is not without interest.
>
> People's loftiest affirmations are not without a similar universality. Our innermost being consists of many vocations; this kind of affirmation is not excluded. People are, in this respect, their highest selves, insofar as they exist in human society.
>
> 25 January 1729
>> Your humble and obedient servant
>> Buarotti

French literary critic Philarète Chasles publishes an essay titled 'Hölderlin, le fou de la Révolution' (Hölderlin, Madman of the Revolution), in which he attributes the poet's madness to a stay in Paris. '*D'un paisible rêveur, Paris fit un insensé . . . jeune, il avait rêvé la paix de la république platonicienne; adolescent, il avait maudit l'Europe esclave. Le voilà fou pour avoir vu Paris. Le monstre civilisateur l'a étouffé* (Paris turned a peaceful dreamer into a fool . . . as a young man, he had dreamt of the peaceful Platonic republic; as an adolescent, he had railed against a slavish Europe. Now he was driven mad for having seen Paris. The 'civilizing monster' has suffocated him.)

Bettina von Arnim publishes the epistolary novel *Die Günderode* (Miss Günderode), which includes many anecdotes from Sinclair (credited as St Clair) about Hölderlin:

> St Clair said . . . that listening to him [Hölderlin] was just like listening to the roar of the wind, for he is always hissing in hymns, and the interruptions are like when the wind turns, and then one can grasp a deeper meaning, and the idea that he is mad completely vanishes . . . Hölderlin once said that everything is rhythm, the whole of human destiny is one celestial rhythm, just as every work of art is a unique rhythm, and everything issues from the poetizing lips of God; and when the human spirit submits, then destinies are transfigured—genius manifests itself in them, and poetry becomes a

struggle for truth, at times in a pliable and athletic spirit, whereby the word grasps the body
(the poetic form), at times in an Hesperian
spirit . . . To me, his sayings are like oracles,
which he pronounces in a state of madness,
serving as the priest of God. Certainly, from his
perspective, all worldly ways of life must seem
like incomprehensible madness.

**10 November.** Feucht, the cobbler, issues an invoice:
For Herr Helderle:

| | |
|---|---|
| 6 August, one shoe repaired, | 12 Kreuzer |
| 4 November, one shoe repaired, | 8 |
| total, | 20 |

# 1841

**14 January.** C. T. Schwab, who had been enrolled at the Tübinger Stift since the autumn of 1840, visits Hölderlin for the first time and records the encounter in his diary:

> Today I finally managed, after a few futile attempts, to meet with Hölderlin. I hadn't tried too hard, because I was torn by the idea that I would destroy the beautiful image I had formed in my head, based on anecdotes from his youth. I now know that the difference is so extreme that both images can coexist without harming each other . . . I walked in, he was sitting at the piano, playing, but immediately stood and paid me a few compliments, which I returned. Although the girl had said he would come out as soon as he saw me, I was thrilled he didn't, instead he sat back down and resumed playing. He played quite melodiously, but without any score. He didn't say a word, and for half an hour I stood by the piano without speaking to him. I could readily take in his physical features—at first, I had difficulty

getting oriented, because I couldn't rid my mind of the handsomely youthful image I had conjured up—but then I focussed and paid no attention to the deep wrinkles on his face. His forehead is high and perfectly vertical, his nose rather plain, perhaps slightly pronounced, but with a straight profile. His mouth is small, his lips are thin and, like his chin and the rest of his lower face, generally very tender looking. Sometimes, particularly when he had performed a melodic passage well, he would look at me: his eyes, which are grey in colour, have an opaque glow, albeit lacking energy, and the whites of his eyes seem so waxy that I grew frightened. I felt such emotion that my eyes filled with tears, and I couldn't help but cry; the fact that I was so moved—which he may have attributed to the music—seemed to please him, and he looked at me a couple of times with childlike candour. I tried as best I could to let reason control my gaze, and to preserve a naturally decorous demeanour, which might have helped me grow more friendly with him. At last, I ventured to ask whether I might see his room, which he agreed to, and opened the door, saying, 'Here, please, Your Majesty.'

I walked in, praised the view, and he concurred.
He looked me over, and said in a low voice a
couple of times to himself, 'He is a general', and
then, 'He's so well dressed' (I happened to be
wearing a silk jacket) . . . I asked him if he had
written *Hyperion* when he was still a student and,
after stammering some nonsense, he nodded.
I asked him if he had ever met Hegel, to which
he nodded as well, adding some incomprehensible words, among which I made out 'the
Absolute' . . . I also asked him about Schiller,
about whom he seemed not to want to hear a
word. The second edition of *Hyperion* was on a
shelf, and I showed him the passages that
enchanted me most, he again displayed approval,
all the more so since he seemed to like my
admiration. I asked him to read me a passage,
but he only pronounced gibberish, the word
*Pallaksh* seems to mean 'yes' . . . Going through
his books, I found Kampe's *Doctrine of the Soul*
and the poems of Klopstock, Zachariä [*sic*] and
Hagedorn. I asked him how he was, and he
assured me he was well; when I remarked that
in such fine a place one couldn't fall ill, he
replied: 'I understand, Sir, I understand.'

**21 January.** C. T. Schwab writes of another visit in his diary:

> On 16 January I visited Hölderlin. During the
> night and that morning, he had been in a bad
> mood. But at two o'clock in the afternoon,
> when I visited him in somewhat calmer
> weather, he was relatively serene. He looked at
> me several times with a friendly expression, but
> his bad mood periodically returned. I laughed
> and told him that he was moody and obstinate,
> and that he often spoke his thoughts out loud,
> which he seemed to accept without any aud-
> ible reply. I remarked on the river flowing so
> magnificently beneath him and the beautiful
> evening, and he replied: 'So you understand me,
> too.' He never addressed anyone by their first
> name but simply said what he thought to him-
> self aloud. While I was reading his *Hyperion*, he
> said to himself: 'Don't look into it so much, it's
> cannibalistic.' When I asked him to sit with me
> on the sofa, he said: 'Under no circumstances,
> it would be dangerous', and then didn't do a
> thing. When I opened the book of his poems,
> he insisted that I not do so, and when I offered
> to lend him Wieland's poems, he absolutely

refused. When standing up or walking away, a couple of times he looked at me and said: 'You have an utterly Slavoyackic face', and 'The Baron is handsome' . . . I went back again today to collect some poems he had written. There were two, and neither had any signature. Zimmer's daughter told me to ask him to write the name Hölderlin underneath. I did, but then he grew enraged, began running around the room, grabbed a chair and impetuously plopped it down in one spot, then moved it to another, all the while shouting incomprehensible words, among which I clearly heard 'My name is Scardanelli'. He finally sat down and furiously scrawled the name Scardanelli below each poem.

The two poems signed Scardanelli are titled 'Höheres Leben' and 'Höhere Menschheit':

### Höheres Leben

*Der Mensch erwählt sein Leben, sein Beschliessen,*
*Von Irrtum frei kennt Weisheit er, Gedanken,*
*Erinnrungen, die in der Welt versanken,*
*Und nichts kann ihm der innern Wert verdriessen.*
*Die prächtige Natur verschönet seine Tage,*

*Der Geist in ihm gewährt ihm neues Trachten*
*In seinem Innern oft, und das, die Wahrheit achten,*
*Und höhern Sinn, und manche seltne Frage.*
*Dann kann der Mensch des Leben Sinn auch kennen,*
*Das Höchste seinem Zweck, das Herrlichste benennen,*
*Gemäss der Menschheit so des Lebens Welt betrachten,*
*Und hohen Sinn als höhres Leben achten.*

## A Higher Life

A person chooses their life, their decisions,
Freed from error, they grasp wisdom, thoughts,
Memories otherwise lost to the world,
And nothing can perturb their inner worth.
Resplendent Nature beautifies their days,
Their spirit preserves new intentions within
Their innermost self and ensures they tend to
    truth,
and a higher purpose, and the occasional rare
    question.
And a person can know the meaning of life,
They can call their goals the highest, magnificent,
And consider the living world by the measure of
    humanity
and tend to a high purpose as a higher life.

### Höhere Menschheit

*Den Menschen ist der Sinn ins Innere gegeben,*
*Dass sie als anerkannt das Bessre wählen,*
*Es gilt als Ziel, es ist das wahre Leben,*
*Von dem sich geistiger des Lebens Jahre zählen.*

### A Higher Humanity

People are given wisdom in their innermost
    being,
So that they recognize the best course, and
    choose it,
That's a worthy goal, a life that is true,
Whereby one's years of life count more
    spiritually.

**24 January.** Sophie Schwab writes to Kerner:

Our Christoph . . . has befriended Hölderlin,
who seems to take a real interest in him, or at
least Christoph has had more success than
others. At Christoph's request, Hölderlin has
written some poems; my darling has read them
and says that Hölderlin's genius still shows
through in them. I look forward to reading
these poems myself . . . Have you read Bettina's
new book, *Die Günderode*? It, too, has many

255

details about Hölderlin there that are interesting . . . I should like to add how wonderful it
is to see how, in Hölderlin, even after forty
years of deep madness, his spirit is still present
and shines through his work after such a long
time.

**26 January.** C. T. Schwab writes in his diary:

Today I visited Hölderlin again . . . I offered
him a cigar, which he accepted, so we walked
around for a while smoking together. He was
quite calm and said clearly comprehensible
things. To whatever I said he usually replied:
'You may be right', 'You are right', and once
he even said, 'That is certainly true.' I told him
I had just received a letter from Athens, and he
listened very carefully as I spoke, then agreed
with what I had said. I asked him about
Matthison, and whether he loved him, and he
nodded; I had known Matthison when I was a
child, and so I asked about him again, but he
only gave highly convoluted answers, and I
soon realized that he was in fact talking about
me. He called me Pater today, and at one point
said, 'You are a very pleasant person . . . '. When
he dropped his handkerchief and I picked it up,

he marvelled at my kindness and cried out,
'Oh, most gracious sir.'

**27 January.** Cotta writes to Karl Gok:

> We have the honour of informing you that we
> intend to publish a set of complete poems, in
> the same format as Schiller's, which we enclose
> here . . . We therefore take the liberty of asking
> you what fee you might charge for Hölderlin's
> poems, and whether you might provide any of
> the deceased's [*sic*!] friends with the materials
> or family details needed to write a brief bio-
> graphical note, which we would like to include
> in the new edition of Hölderlin's poems.

**Mid-February.** Responding to a letter dated 12
February, Gok asks for the same fee as for the first
edition, and suggests Gustav Schwab as a potential
contributor of the brief biographical note, but adds:

> I and all the poet's other relatives wish to take
> this opportunity to staunchly refute the false
> reports that have been circulating in the press
> for some years now. Waiblinger and a few other
> young hacks [he had initially written *lausbuben*,
> 'rascals'] scrawled misleading tidbits regarding
> Hölderlin's fate, and thus far the only thing that

has held us back was our reluctance to be forced into public debate of this matter, which we naturally wish to avoid out of respect for poor Hölderlin. For this reason, I insist that only such information as comes from Hölderlin's letters or other reliable sources be published.

**25 February.** C.T. Schwab writes in his diary:

On 12 February I spent a few minutes with Hölderlin in the afternoon, to give him a copy of his book of poems, since his own copy, which included a few extra pages with new poems, had been stolen.

When I showed it to him, he appreciated the binding but didn't want to accept the gift, although I insisted that he couldn't return it to me. No sooner had I left than he came out of his own room and went into the carpenter's wife's room, which he never used to do in the afternoons. The carpenter's daughter met to him at the door, he handed her the book, and asked her to give it back to the lord baron, as she said she would as soon as I returned. This seemed to satisfy him, and he replied: 'I believe so' . . .

Today I returned and learned that Hölderlin
had not wanted to accept the book. So I went
to him and asked him to write a few lines on
one of the blank pages inside, which he promised to do. He remembered having already
given me a couple of poems, and seemed flattered when I told him that they   had sparked
in me a desire to have more work by him . . . I
showed him the portrait of Waiblinger in the
first volume of his works and when I asked if
he'd known him, he nodded. I then asked
whether, before his death, Waiblinger had
visited often, to which he replied, 'So he's no
longer alive?' . . . Zimmer's daughter told me
that someone had shown him the new litho-
graphic edition of Schiller's works, which had
brought him great joy; he had liked the scenes
from *Wallenstein* in particular (also, in my
opinion, the best) and had said: 'That man is
without compare.' In general, he's still very
intelligent and can pass reasonable judgments
when it comes to art. As soon as I left, they
brought him pen and ink, and he sat down to
write in the book.

**16 February.** A contract is signed between 'Mr Councillor Gok, on behalf of his brother, Master Librarian Hoelderlin' and the publisher Cotta for the publication of Hölderlin's poems 'in an elegant paperback edition'.

**21 April.** Gok sends Schwab materials for a biography of Hölderlin, adding:

> Considering that you will find much material here that contradicts the shallow biographies drafted by Waiblinger and others, and that it will be of some interest to you to learn more about Hölderlin's noble character through reliable correspondence, I have decided to send to you a portion of my own cache of letters [from Hölderlin himself] as evidence, which I have, thus far, guarded like precious treasure . . . I have no objection to including a letter from Hölderlin's dear friend Sinclair . . . which provides some clarifications regarding his relationship with a late female friend. I trust that you will treat this tender relationship, which doubtless had the saddest influence on the unfortunate man, with all the delicacy that this noble object of Hölderlin's veneration and his surviving family deserve.

**13 May.** Gok contacts the Zimmer family and suggests that he could send them a portion of the forthcoming publication fee to cover a daily 'snack', which 'my unfortunate brother ... now in his old age, will need— in addition to the usual food'. He also asks that a doctor be consulted, to ensure that 'a snack every day, between breakfast, the midday meal and the evening meal with a hearty glass of well-aged wine, would be tolerable and adequate for Hölderlin at his advanced age'.

**24 May.** Lotte Zimmer writes to Frau Gok:

> Your brother-in-law has been unwell for a couple of weeks, he is quite congested, because at night he often leaves his room barefoot. He caught a cold, so I got up one night and made him tea, and now he is well again, it's just that at night he is restless, and I have to tell him to relax, and remind him no one else can sleep unless he calms down. The current cold spell certainly affects him.
>
> I am sending you the requested certificate, with a doctor's opinion from Professor Gmelin. I don't know if it fits what you were looking for, Gmelin says he doesn't consider straight wine advisable, it might be too strong ... As you can read is his certificate, the professor also

wonders whether the fee for food should be increased, which I have declined to do several times already . . . please, rest assured that you brother-in-law receives good food befitting to his needs, and when I cook up something special for my mother he receives the same, that is why we want to leave everything as before, and only add a little something in the evenings . . . Every day in the morning and at midday he receives a glass with three parts wine and one part of our home-made drink, which is always very good and pure, because we make it with grape must, not watered down, and he gladly drinks it, it's healthy and does him no harm. Each morning I make him something hot, and I also offer him something from the oven, and when I can I sometimes give him bread and butter.

**18 July.** According to Schwab, Hölderlin writes the following untitled poem:

> *Des Geistes Werden ist den Menschen nicht verborgen,*
> *Und wie das Leben ist, das Menschen sich gefunden,*
> *Es ist des Lebens Tag, es ist des Lebens Morgen,*
> *Wie Reichtum sind des Geistes hohe Stunden.*
> *Wie die Natur sich dazu herrlich findet,*

*Ist, dass der Mensch nach solcher Freude schauet,*
*Wie er dem Tage sich, dem Leben sich vertrauet,*
*Wie er mit sich den Bund des Geistes bindet.*

The becoming of the spirit is not hidden from
    humans,
Nor is the life people find themselves living,
'Tis the day of life, 'tis the morning of life,
The spirit's high hours are like riches.
Just as Nature is magnificent indeed,
People seek out a similar joy,
Just as they commit themselves to the day, to life,
Just as they make a pact of the spirit.

**25 July.** Marie Nathusius writes in her diary:

Philipp asked young Schwab, who is a student
here, if he could arrange for us an opportunity
to see Hölderlin . . . He took us to the room
of a friend of his, who lives in the same house
as Hölderlin, and where he often goes to play
the piano . . . We waited anxiously, then heard
him descend the stairs. The door opened, and
in walked an old man—he's now 70—in his
dressing gown, his thin hair groomed simply,
his head inclined, albeit more out of reserve
than weakness. He took a few deep bows.

Schwab said we were his admirers and asked if
he would be so good as to play us a little something. With still more bows and words like 'Your
Majesty, Your Holiness' he sat down at the piano
and began to play. We stood close by, deeply
moved by the sad sight: the inspired young poet
was now a doddering old man; his forehead
had once housed deep spiritual intuitions, his
enraptured eyes had once contemplated vast
beauty, but now every part of him looked confused and unsteady. Only now and then did his
features appear sweetly melancholic. Sometimes
he still writes poems, about single, deep, and
wonderful thoughts, albeit entirely without
coherence [*ohne Zusammenhang*].

**10 August.** A civil servant named Zeller—who had
become Hölderlin's guardian as soon as his predecessor,
Burk, grew old enough to retire—writes to Gok:

> I felt it was my duty to personally ascertain the
> condition of the unfortunate man, who had
> once nurtured such high hopes and whose sad
> state no one can disregard. I am convinced that
> the accommodation he is living in is suitable
> in every respect, and that he is being treated in
> an absolutely adequate manner. According to

Frau Zimmer's report, it has been decided the sick man shall receive a supplement of wine or hot drinks twice a day, starting on 22 May, for a total of 8 Kreuzer additional expenditure. Not only do I feel obliged to confirm this decision—as the resources for his subsistence are more than sufficient—but I also feel obliged, since we cannot give the ailing man any greater spiritual sustenance, to provide any and everything that he might enjoy.

**Autumn** (presumably). Johann Georg Fischer, who studied in Tübingen from 1841 to 1843, visits Hölderlin several times. He later publishes a series of accounts from these visits, including one about the first time he met the poet:

On my first visit I was accompanied by Professor Auberlen from Basel, and when we arrived at the door, we heard Hölderlin passionately improvising at the piano. My heart was pounding, and when we knocked a hoarse yet loud 'come in' rang out. Hölderlin responded to our greetings with a deep bow and gestures inviting us to sit down. He wore a damask dressing gown and slippers. There was no sense introducing ourselves, because he had already addressed one of us as 'Your Holiness' and the other as 'Your Majesty'. When we addressed him as 'Herr Doktor' we were immediately corrected: 'Librarian' . . . In those first few anguished moments of the long-anticipated encounter with a mind so extraordinary, albeit in its misfortune so elusive, the conversation on our side was understandably awkward and fearful. But I shall never forget how his face suddenly brightened when a question resonated or a name struck him. When I steered the conversation towards his first encounters with Schiller, which clearly awakened memories of his young friend, his blue eyes looked up and he cried out: 'Ah, Schiller, my magnificent Schiller!' But when the conversation turned to Goethe, his expression seemed to grow cold, almost annoyed, and he merely said: 'Ah, Herr Goethe!'

**25 December.** Hölderlin writes and (presumably correctly) dates one of several poems titled 'Der Winter':

### Der Winter

*Wenn sich das Laub auf Ebnen weit verloren,*
*So fällt das Weiss herunter auf die Tale,*
*Doch glänzend ist der Tag vom hohen Sonnenstrahle,*

*Es glänzt das Fest den Städten aus den Toren.*
*Es ist die Ruhe der Natur, des Feldes Schweigen*
*Ist wie des Menschen Geistigkeit, und höher zeigen*
*Die Unterschiede sich, dass sich zu hohem Bilde*
*Sich zeiget die Natur, statt mit des Frühlings Milde.*
*d. 25 Dezember 1841*

> *Der unterthänigster*
> *Scardanelli*

**Winter**
When foliage drops away on the distant plain
A white mantle falls on the valley,
And the day shines bright with rays from on high,
Cities' gates are resplendent in festival.
Nature is at rest, the fields fall silent,
People grow soulful, life's diversities
Ever greater, and Nature herself is revealed
in an image from on high, instead of mild spring.
25 December 1841

> Your most subservient
> Scardanelli

**1 December.** Seeger, the furrier, issues an invoice:

For Herr Librarian Hölderlin:

A chamber cap with green cloth

> 1 Gulden 20 Kreuzer

# 1842

**22 January.** at Zeller's request, Gmelin attests that Hölderlin is still mentally ill:

> I certify that magister Hölderlin, residing here [in Tübingen], is still in a state of mental illness [*in geisteskranken Zustände*].
>
> Tübingen, 22 Jan. 1842
>
> Professor Dr F. G. Gmelin

At some point during this same month, according to a manuscript annotation by C. T. Schwab, Hölderlin composed a poem titled 'Winter':

> *Das Feld ist kahl, auf ferner Höhe glänzet*
> *Der blaue Himmel nur, und wie die Pfade gehen,*
> *Erscheinet die Natur, als Einerlei, das Wehen*
> *Ist frisch, und die Natur von Helle nur umkränzet.*
> *Der Erde Stund ist sichtbar von dem Himmel*
> *Den ganzen Tag, in heller Nacht umgeben,*
> *Wenn hoch erscheint von Sternen das Gewimmel,*
> *Und geistiger das weit gedehnte Leben.*

The field lies bare, atop the distant heights
Solely blue sky gleams, and as the footpaths go
Nature appears all the same, the winds grow

Brisk, and Nature is wreathed in lights.
The earthly hour is visible from the heavens
The whole day long, surrounded by night,
    splendid
When the teeming stars appear on high,
And more spiritual this human life, extended.

**18 January.** Moriz Carrière writes to Cotta:

I take the liberty of pointing you to a poet
whose works have been issued by your publishing house, whose small readership I would
like to grow . . . I'm referring to Hölderlin,
prophet of a more beautiful future for both
Church and State, the greatest living elegiac
poet. His Sophocles should certainly be combined with *Hyperion* and his poems, and the
latter would need to be completed for the new
edition . . . Arnim published a great poem,
comparable to Novalis' *Hymns to the Night*, in
a journal in Berlin. An introduction should be
added, especially to elucidate the meaning of
*Hyperion* . . .

**19 April.** Lotte Zimmer writes to Zeller:

Your ward felt unwell for a few days, although
now he is better, so I went to see Gmelin, who

examined him but didn't prescribe anything. He had a lot of phlegm, as well as a nosebleed, and the doctor said that the bleeding is very good for him, we just need to be very careful with his food and drink. He also had a fever, so I gave him lemonade instead of wine, several times a day, which helped. In general, you can rest assured he has everything he needs, and I work to ensure that nothing is neglected . . . I wouldn't want to have any regrets, or anything weighing on my conscience, if he were to leave this world. I am determined that we be able to say we treated the poor soul generously, never with the slightest selfishness, which unfortunately happens so often among us mere mortals. We must also replace the bed linens . . .

**Late Spring.** Louise Keller, a friend of C. T. Schwab's, visits Hölderlin and draws a pencil portrait of him, to be used as the frontispiece for a forthcoming edition of his poems.

**30 June.** During a soirée at Gustav Schwab's house, an eyewitness speaks of the aforementioned drawing, as well as the conversation regarding Hölderlin among those present:

This friend [Louise Keller] had just returned from Tübingen, where, thanks to Christoph Schwab . . . she had been invited to the ailing poet's home. Once there, she managed to make a drawing of him, the first and last picture preserved. We passed it around the room. I can still see Lenau staring at it for a long time . . . Later that same evening, other details of Hölderlin's last days were described: how, in order not to offend him, he had to be addressed as 'Librarian', how he often addressed others as 'Your Holiness', and how the name 'Thekla' began showing up increasingly often in his horribly broken sentences, along with words in French . . . In the last few weeks Uhland had sent him a vase with flowers. Hölderlin received it with joy and admiration, exclaiming 'These flowers are splendiferously Asian [*prachtasiatische*].'

**13 July.** The theology student Ferdinand Schimpf reports:

Habermas, a fellow student who lived in Zimmer's house, gave me and my friend Keller the opportunity to see and speak to the mad poet Hölderlin, whom he had invited to his

room one afternoon for coffee. On this occa-
sion, the poor poet wrote these verses for us,
ex tempore, upon our request. If we called him
by his first name, he refused to answer to it,
instead replying, 'You are speaking to Mr
Rosetti.' He was incredibly complimentary.

## Der Herbst

*Das Glänzen der Natur ist höheres Erscheinen,*
*Wo sich der Tag mit vielen Freuden endet,*
*Es ist das Jahr das sich mit Pracht vollendet,*
*Wo Früchte sich mit frohem Glanz vereinen.*
*Das Erdenrund ist so geschmückt, und selten lärmet*
*Der Schall durchs offne Feld, die Sonne wärmet*
*Den tag des Herbstes mild, die Felder stehen*
*Als eine Aussicht weit, die Lüfte wehen*
*Die Zweig und Äste durch mit frohem Rauschen,*
*Wenn schon mit Leere sich die Felder dann*
      *vertauschen,*
*Der ganze Sinn des hellen Bildes lebet*
*Als wie ein Bild, das goldne Pracht umschwebet.*

## Autumn

Nature's radiance is higher revelation,
Where with many joys the day draws to its end,
'Tis the year itself, in glorious consummation,

**15.** L. Keller, Portrait of Hölderlin, 1842.

Where fruits with joyous resplendence blend.
Earth's globe is duly adorned, less often do
    alarms
Ring out through the open field, the sun
    gently warms
The autumnal day, the far fields are on show
Like broad views, the breezes blow
Through twigs and branches, rustling with
    cheerfulness,
When the fields trade places with an emptiness.
The full significance of this bright image
    lives, like
A painting ringed by golden light.

**20 July.** Lotte Zimmer writes to Zeller:

> A few days ago he [Hölderlin] grew angry
> because he had slammed the window too hard,
> and he came to me in great distress, insisting
> that I see the damage. I asked whether he had
> done it, and he replied that he couldn't say for
> sure, that the wind might have done it, and his
> denial made me smile. When the window was
> repaired, he said, 'You're so kind to me'; it's
> funny how he takes it to heart when he breaks
> something, and gets very upset about it . . .

**Summer (likely 28 July).** The medical doctor and philosopher Heinrich Czolbe, who 'as a student felt great sympathy for the poet of *Hyperion*', visits Hölderlin. As his biographer later testified, 'The conversation moved him deeply, and left a lasting impression on the young man's soul. As he wandered through the beautiful Neckar valley, he resolved to work with all his might to ensure that the poet's ideal would be realised, that a more harmonious form of life would be achieved, and that a serene, natural religion would drive out all vain impulses of sad fanaticism.'

Hölderlin probably writes the following poem for Czolbe:

*Wenn aus sich lebt der Mensch und wenn sein Rest*
     *sich zeiget,*
*So ists, als wenn ein Tag sich Tagen unterscheidet,*
*Dass ausgezeichnet sich der Mensch zum Reste neiget,*
*Von der Natur getrennt und unbeneidet.*
*Als wie allein ist er im andern weiten Leben,*
*Wo rings der Frühling grünt, der Sommer freundlich*
     *weilet,*
*Bis dass das Jahr im Herbst hinunter eilet,*
*Und immerdar die Wolken uns umschweben.*
*d. 28 Juli 1842*

               *mit Unterthnigkeit*
               *Scardanelli*

When one lives on their own and their vestiges
    are revealed,
'Tis as if a day were to divide itself from other
    days
And, magnificent, one bows down to those
    vestiges,
Entirely divided from nature, and unenvied.
It's as if they're all alone in that other vast life,
Where springtime bursts into verdure, and
    summer lingers
Sweetly, until the year dives into autumn
And clouds envelop us for evermore.
28 July 1842
            Your humble and obedient servant,
                       Scardanelli

**30 September.** Gustav Schwab writes to Cotta: 'I am pleased to send you the most recently corrected drafts of Hölderlin's poems, as well as the biographical note . . . My son has expressed to me his wish that one copy of these poems be produced without the biographical profile.'

**24 October.** The second edition of the poems is published.

**7 November.** Hölderlin writes another poem titled 'Winter':

*Wenn ungesehn und nun vorüber sind die Bilder*
*Der Jahreszeit, so kommt des Winters Dauer,*
*Das Feld is leer, die Ansicht scheinet milder,*
*Und Stürme wehn umher und Regenschauer.*
*Als wie ein Ruhetag, so ist des Jahres Ende,*
*Wie einer Frage Ton, dass dieser sich vollende,*
*Als dann erscheint des Frühlings neues Werden,*
*So glänzet die Natur mit ihrer Pracht auf Erden.*
*d. 24 April 1849*

> *Mit Unterthänigkeit*
> *Scardanelli*

When the season's images have passed unseen,
Long Winter comes our way again;
The field lies bare, the view has a milder sheen,
And gales blow about us, bringing showers
    of rain.
Like a day of rest comes the year's conclusion,
Like the tone of a question seeking completion;
Thereupon comes the advent of Spring,
Thus Nature shines resplendent upon everything.
24 April 1849

> Your humble and obedient servant,
> Scardanelli

**27 November.** Zeller is replaced by Dr Essig as Hölderlin's guardian.

According to Karl Rosenkranz, the phrase *en kai pan*, which Hölderlin had also written in Hegel's guestbook, 'can still be seen today, on a large sheet of paper, posted on the wall of his room in Tübingen'.

**2 December.** Feucht, the tailor, issues an invoice:

For Herr Librarian Helderle:

| | |
|---|---|
| Made a lined pair of trousers, | 54 |
| buttons, | 12 |
| linen fabric, | 55 |
| mended a dressing gown, | 10 |
| total | 2 Gulden 17 |

# 1843

**January (likely the 24th).** Uhland and the Germanist Adelbert Keller, together with Christoph Schwab, visit the poet, whom they find 'content and serene', but who also 'inspires a reverential awe'. Hölderlin writes 'a poem about winter' for them, with 'beautiful images and thoughts', but 'without coherence' (*ohne Zusammenhang*). This is presumably one of several poems titled 'Winter', two of which are dated 24 January 1676 and 24 January 1743, respectively.

## Der Winter

*Wenn sich das Jahr geändert, und der Schimmer*
*Der prächtigen Natur vorüber, blühet nimmer*
*Der Glanz des Jahreszeit, und schneller eilen*
*Die Tage dann vorbei, die langsam auch verweilen.*
*Der Geist des Lebens ist verschieden in den Zeiten*
*Der lebenden Natur, verschiedne Tage breiten*
*Das Glänzen aus, und immerneues Wesen*
*Erscheint den Menschen recht, vorzüglich und erlesen.*
*d. 24 Januar 1676*

*Mit Unterthänigkeit*
*Scardanelli*

## Winter

When the year changes and the glimmer is gone
When Nature's magnificence flourishes no more
The season's resplendence swiftly passes, as do
the days, which also slowly drag on.
The spirit of life is different in times when
Nature is alive, when varied days unfurl
their splendour, and ever-newer ways of being
strike people as right, preferable and chosen.
24 January 1676
        Your humble and obedient servant,
                    Scardanelli

## Der Winter

*Wenn sich der Tag des Jahrs hinabgeneiget*
*Und rings das Feld mit den Gebirgen schweiget,*
*So glänzt das Blau des Himmels an den Tagen,*
*Die wie Gestirn in heitrer Höhe ragen.*
*Der Wechsel und die Pracht ist minder umgebreitet,*
*Dort, wo ein Strom hinab mit Eile gleitet,*
*Der Ruhe Geist ist aber in den Stunden*
*Der prächtigen Natur mit Tiefigkeit verbunden.*
*d. 24 Januar 1743*
               *Mit Unterthänigkeit*
                 *Scardanelli*

**Winter**

When the day of the year reaches its end,
And surrounding fields and mountains fall silent,
A heavenly blue shines brightly through the
    days,
Which are, like stars, on high arrayed.
Change and splendour become less widespread
Where rivers' currents swiftly flow downward,
But a peaceful spirit can be found in the hours,
When glorious nature is bound to great depth.
24 January 1743
                    Your humble and obedient servant,
                                              Scardanelli

**27 January** (or in early December of the previous year,
just after the second edition of the poems was released).
Johann Georg Fischer visits Hölderlin again:

A later visit made a significant impression on
us. It took place immediately after the edition
of Hölderlin's poems in miniature, and I was
with Auberlen and Christoph Schwab—Gustav
Schwab's son, who subsequently became editor
of Cotta's edition of Hölderlin's works, as well
as a professor in Stuttgart. He gave Hölderlin a
copy of this new edition, which he quickly
leafed through, and thanked Schwab with a

nod. Then, looking once more at the title, he said: 'Yes, the poems are authentic [*echte*], they are mine [*sie sind von mir*], but the name is wrong; I have never in my life been called Hölderlin, I go by Scardanelli or Scaliger Rosa . . .'. When Auberlen asked him, 'Herr Librarian, sir, you've also worked on Sophocles, haven't you?', he answered, 'I tried to translate *Oedipus*, but the publisher was a . . . ' whereupon he uttered a profanity, and repeated the insult several times. I then turned to him and said: 'But your *Hyperion* was a success, and your venerated Diotima was a noble creation.' At this his face lit up, and he replied, counting on his fingers: 'Ah, my Diotima! Don't talk to me about my Diotima; she gave me thirteen children. One became pope, another became a sultan, and the third is emperor of Russia.' And then he added, in Swabian dialect, 'And you know what happened? He went mad, mad mad mad!' [*Ond wisset Se, wies no ganga ischt? Närret ischt se worde, närret, närret*]. He repeated this last word so violently, with such vehement gestures, that we couldn't bear it any longer, and put an end to his crisis by taking our leave. He saluted us, as always, with 'I remain your devoted servant.'

(Note the shift from language to dialect, as if to underline the conscious, perhaps staged madness of the previous words).

**30 January.** Lotte Zimmer writes to Dr Essig: '... I could not enclose the receipt for the dressing gown because the tailor has not yet finished his work ... your ward is currently very well, this time he is having a very good winter ... '.

**6 February.** Mörike writes to Wilhelm Hartlaub about his visit to Hölderlin's sister, Professor Breunlin's widow, 'a very talkative lady', in Nürtingen:

> She showed me several portraits of Hölderlin, including a large pastel he had sent her for her wedding [and gave me] a large basket full of Hölderlin's manuscripts. The lady of the house warmed up a little attic room for me, where the oldest furniture and family pictures are, so that I could examine the manuscripts without being disturbed. I sat there all alone, but every now and then the maidservant would come in with her knitting. This provided a very necessary distraction, otherwise one would lose one's mind when faced with such a pile of rubble.

GIORGIO AGAMBEN

I found noteworthy drafts of his poems
(most printed), with many corrections; often
they were variants or transcriptions of the
same poem (Schwab, as I could see from his
annotations, used these papers for his rather
diligent edition, as far as I could judge).
There were translations from Sophocles (some
printed), Euripides and Pindar; essays on
dramaturgy; letters from lesser-known friends
(Siegfr. Schmid, Neuffer et al.), as well as some
in Hölderlin's own hand and, if my conjecture
is correct, an outline of the woman we know
as Diotima; sheets from the first edition of
*Hyperion*, which looked as if they had just
come off press. Particularly touching were
various little scraps of paper from his time in
Homburg and Jena, which abruptly transported me to the very start of his unfortunate
present-day state of existence.

**March.** Arnold Runge writes to Karl Marx:

It is harsh, and yet I must say it, for it is the
truth: I cannot imagine any other people who
are as torn apart as the German people. You see
craftsmen, but no true humans; thinkers, but no
true humans; lords and servants, young and old,

but no true humans. Is this not a battlefield,
where hands, arms and all limbs lie separate,
torn asunder, while their lifeblood seeps out
into the sand?' So writes Hölderlin in his
*Hyperion.*This motto perfectly captures my state
of mind and, unfortunately, it is nothing new.

**20 March.** According to some, around this date—his
birthday—Hölderlin composes the poem 'Spring':

### Der Frühling

*Wenn aus der Tiefe kommt der Frühling in das Leben,*
*Es wundert sich der Mensch, und neue Worte streben*
*aus Geistigkeit, die Freude kehret wieder*
*Und festlich machen sich Gesang und Lieder.*
*Das Leben findet sich aus Harmonie der Zeiten,*
*Dass immerdar den Sinn Natur und Geist geleiten.*
*Und die Vollkommenheit ist Eines in dem Geiste,*
*So findet vieles sich, und aus Natur das Meiste.*
*d. 24 Mai 1758*

*Mit Unterthänigkeit*
*Scardanelli*

### Spring

When, from the depths, springtime comes to life,
People marvel, and new words grow rife,
Moved by the spirit, joy returns once more

And both song and singing festively roar.
Life is found in seasonal harmony, such that
Nature and Spirit might always accompany
    thought,
And Perfection is One in mind and heart;
Such that, from Nature most of all, much is
    brought.
24 May 1758

> Your humble and obedient servant,
> Scardanelli

**April.** Fischer visits Hölderlin for the last time:

I went with two other colleagues in theology, Brandauer and Ostertag, in April 1843. I told Hölderlin that I had come to see him to take my leave because I had to leave Tübingen, which he did not accept. We weren't sure whether he remembered me or my friends from previous visits, because each time he received us with his usual detachment, no facial expression seemed to hint that he recalled our previous encounters. On this last visit I asked him: 'Herr Librarian, I would be delighted if you would give me a couple of verses, as a token of farewell.' He replied: 'As His Holiness commands! Shall I write about

Greece, spring, or the spirit of the age?' My friends whispered: 'The spirit of the age!' So I asked for that.

Then the perpetually stooped man sat down at his desk, back straight as a board, picked up some paper and a full-feather quill, and prepared to write. Until the day I die, I shall never forget his face at that radiant moment. His eyes and forehead seemed to glow, as if they had never known any heavy mental confusion. He proceeded to write, tapping out the metre of each verse with his left hand, and at the end of each one a satisfied *Hm!* rose from his chest. When he had finished, he handed me the paper, took a deep bow, and said, 'May Your Holiness deign to accept?' I offered my final thanks with a handshake. I would never see him again. In May I left Tübingen, and in June he was buried. The verses he gave me, which were later taken from me by an avid collector, go like this:

*Der Zeitgeist*

*Die Menschen finden sich in dieser Welt zum Leben,*
*Wie Jahre sind, wie Zeiten höher streben,*
*So wie de Wechsel ist, ist übrig vieles Wahre,*

*Dass Dauer kommt in die verschiednen Jahre;*
*Vollkommenheit vereint sich so in diesem Leben,*
*Dass diesem sich bequemt der Menschen edles Streben.*
d. 24 Mai 1748

Mit Unterthänigkeit<br>Scardanelli

### The Spirit of the Age

People have been put in this world to live,
They're like years, like ages, times striving higher,
Just as so much changes, so much truth remains,
Longevity comes over varying years;
Thus perfection unites within this life,
Such that it shapes people's noblest aims.
24 May 1748

Your humble and obedient servant,<br>Scardanelli

**Early June.** Hölderlin writes what is believed to be his last poem:

### Die Aussicht

*Wenn in die Ferne geht der Menschen wohnend*
    *Leben,*
*Wo in die Ferne sich erglänzt die Zeit der Reben*
*Ist auch dabei des Sommers leer Gefilde,*
*Der Wald erscheint mit seinem dunklen Bilde;*

*Dass die Natur ergänzt das Bild der Zeiten,*
*Dass die verweilt, sie schnell vorübergleiten,*
*Ist aus volkommenheit, des Himmels Höhe glänzet*
*Dem Menschen dann, wie Bäume Blüht' umkränzet.*
*d. 24 Mai 1748*

> *Mit Unterthänigkeit*
> *Scardanelli*

**The View**

When one's life of dwelling goes off into
    the distance,
Where, faraway, the vineyard's season glistens,
There, too, summer's empty fields draw near,
The woods and their dark countenances appear.
That Nature completes the image of the ages,
That it lingers as they glide by, swiftly turning
    pages
Is sheer perfection, and the high heavens shine
For people, too, like trees crowned in flowers
    so fine.
24 May 1748

> Your humble and obedient servant,
> Scardanelli

**7 June.** Lotte Zimmer writes Karl Gok:

Most esteemed Herr Councillor,

I have the honour of informing you of the very sad news of the passing of your beloved brother. He had been coughing and had a lot of phlegm for a few days. We noticed a particular weakness in him, so I went to see Dr Gmelin, who gave him some medicine. That evening he played piano again and had dinner in our room, and at night he went to bed, but then he got up and told me that he was too anxious to stay in bed. I spoke to him and stayed by his side, and after a few minutes he took some more medicine, but he continued to grow more and more anxious. Another guest staying in our house was also beside him, while another guest his commotion had woken was next to me, and he died so gently and peacefully, without any agony. My mother was also at his side, and none of us had expected such a swift death. Our grief is now so great that it is beyond tears, and yet we must thank our Heavenly Father a thousand times over that he did not suffer; few men have ever died as gently as your dear brother did.

In his biography, C. T. Schwab describes Hölderlin's death as follows:

> Suddenly one evening he felt very ill. He went to the open window seeking relief and gazed out for a long time at the beautiful full moon, which seemed to calm him down, but in the meantime his exhaustion increased, and he went to bed. Here he immediately felt death approaching . . .

The Tübinger Stift church register contains the following details:

> Friedrich Hölderlin, Librarian, Poet,
>    *mente absens* for about 40 years.

> Parents: †Heinrich Fried. Hölderlin,
> administrator
>    †Johanne Christiane née Heyn

> Date of birth and age: 29 March 1770,
>    73 years old

> Illness: pulmonary paralysis

> Date of death and burial: 7 June, 10.45 p.m.
>    and 10 June at 10 a.m.

**11 June.** Gmelin writes Karl Gok:

I thought it very important to his friends that I examine the corpse and hoped to hear your opinion; but because I received no reply, the autopsy took place in the presence of my son and Dr Rapp, yielding interesting results. The brain was perfect, well formed, and even perfectly sound, with the exception of a cavity: the *ventriculus septi pellucidi* was significantly enlarged by water; its walls had thickened and hardened, particularly the *corpus callosum,* the *fornix*, and the lateral walls. As there was otherwise no other abnormality in the brain, this must be regarded as the cause of his forty-year illness, as it certainly put pressure on the most precious part of the brain.

We found both lungs filled with water, which explains his death, which occurred, contrary to most cases of pleural dropsy, very quickly and easily.

We would like to thank God, who called this late pilgrim to Himself in such a gentle and painless way.

N.B. The funeral was very festive and was also attended by many students.

**10 June.** Hölderlin is buried at 10 in the morning in the Tübingen cemetery. The students who lived in Zimmer's house carried the coffin, followed by about a hundred other students. 'Those who had been close to him,' writes C.T. Schwab, who also gave the eulogy, 'mourned him like a brother . . . a large laurel wreath adorned the dead man's head . . . As soon as the coffin was lowered, the clouded sky cleared, and the sun shed its friendly rays on the open grave.' No professors were present. Neither Uhland nor Gustav Schwab attended, and although the decedent's brother and sister were also absent, they inherited 12,259 Gulden from the poet.

**16.** Detail of a text signed 'Scardanelli' in C. T. Schwab's copy of the poetry collection published in 1826.

# EPILOGUE

What is a 'dwelling life' [*vita abitante*]? Certainly, a life lived according to customs and habits [*abiti e abitudini*].[1] The German verb *wohnen* derives from the Indo-European root \**wen-(1)*, which means 'to desire' or 'to strive for'. It is also related to the German words *Wahn* ('delusion'), *Wonne* ('delight'), and to the Latin *venus*. This means that in the German language the acquisition of a habit (*Gewohnheit*) is etymologically associated with pleasure and joy—and, although linguists tend to divide the two terms, delusion (*Wahn*) and madness (*Wahnsinn*).

The verb *wohnen*, which appears with all these various meanings throughout Hölderlin's work, in his poetry generally refers to humans' life on earth. Of

---

1 The *vita abitante* referred to here is the *wohnend Leben* referred to in the first line of what is widely considered Hölderlin's last poem. The German reads 'Wenn in die Ferne geht der Menschen wohnend Leben . . .'; Agamben's Italian version is 'Quando lontano va la vita abitante degli uomini . . .'; I have rendered this in English as 'When one's life of dwelling goes off into the distance . . .' [Trans.]

course the poet uses this same verb for many other things that dwell or inhabit—stars ('Der Frieden', lines 54–55: *Denn ewig wohnen sie, des Aethers / Blühende Sterne*), eagles ('Patmos', lines 5–6: *Im Finstern wohnen / die Adler*), beauty ('Griechenland', third version, lines 43–44: *Daß lieber auf Erden / Die Schönheit wohnt*) and God ('Heimkunft' 2, lines 3–4: *Und noch höher hinauf wohnt über dem Lichte der reine / Seelige Gott*), to name just a few—but that is precisely what brings them closer to the human realm of dwelling [*dimora*]. One of Hölderlin's phrases—which Waiblinger mentions transcribing in his *Phaëthon*, and upon which Heidegger commented at length—appears in the poem 'In lieblicher Bläue' and states unreservedly that 'people dwell poetically on this earth' (*dichterisch, wohnet der Mensch auf dieser Erde*). It is likely that this dictum intentionally echoes a passage of the Lutheran Bible (John 1:14), *das Wort ward Fleisch und wohnte unter uns*, 'the word became flesh, and dwelt among us'. By becoming flesh, God dwells as a human among humans, partaking in the basic fact of dwelling.

Translating the German *wohnen* into Latin leads us to the verb *habito*—from which both the Italian *abitare* and the English *to inhabit* are derived—a frequentative form of *habeo*, 'to have'. Frequentatives express a repeated and intensified action. They are formed by adding the suffix -*ito* to the supine verb stem, i.e. a diathesis (or voice) of the verb in which meaning is expressed with indifference to tense and mode. To quote Émile Benveniste, the term *supine* is 'analogous to the attitude of a carefree man, lying down (the Latin *supinus* translates the Greek *yptios*, meaning "lying on his back")'.[2] An 'inhabiting' (or 'dwelling') life is, therefore, a life that repeatedly and intensively 'has' a certain way of being—that is, as previously mentioned, one lived according to customs and habits. But what kind of continuity and connection binds together repeated, habitual actions? Taking this last form of the Latin stem, a 'habitual' life would therefore be one that has a special continuity and cohesion in relation to itself and to the whole of existence ('habitual', according to Schmidt, refers to 'a life which stands in weaker and more distant relation to everything else'). It is this particular mode of continuity within a life that we need to grasp.

What mode of action or grammatical mood is at issue when one talks about a habit? The late Latin grammarian Charisius distinguishes three types of

2 Émile Benveniste, 'Supinum', *Revue philologique* 58 (1932): 136–37; see also Benveniste, *Noms d'agent et noms d'action en indoeuropéen* (Paris: Maisonneuve, 1948), pp. 100–01.

verbs: active, in which a subject does something; passive, in which a subject undergoes something; and a
third kind, which he calls *habitivum* ('habitual'), in
which the active and passive subject are one and the
same, such that it seems that 'something happens or is
in and of itself [*per se quid fieri aut esse*]'.[3] Another
grammarian, Phocas, built upon Charisius' legacy and
discusses this third type—which the Greeks called
'middle'—using the verbs *gaudeo* ('I enjoy'), *soleo* ('I
usually'), and *fio* ('I become'), and goes on to inform
us that some called these verbs 'supine'. This makes it
clear why Charisius calls them 'habitual' while others
refer to them as 'supine': like the Aristotelian *hexis*
('habit'), such terms indicate a state, process or disposition (*diathesis*) that is not the result of a decision, a wilful
act, nor simply the undergoing of an external action.
Rather, in this case, the subject exists within the process:
it is the place of the event indicated by the verb, which
acts insofar as it undergoes itself—and it does so
supinely, like 'a carefree man, lying down'. This explains
why contemporary linguists speak of *Affiziertheit* or
'affectedness', a condition wherein the subject is
affected in a decisive way by a process in which it is

---

3 Karl Barwick (ed.), *Flavii Sosipatri Charisii Artis grammaticae
libri V.* (Leipzig: Teubner, 1925), pp. 211–12.

neither the active agent nor passive patient—or is actually both, insofar as it is affected by itself (Greek grammarians use the term *synemptosis*, which refers to syncretism or a 'falling together'). Saint Gregory the Great used the expression *secum habitare*, to 'dwell with oneself' or 'dwell within oneself', to describe the life of one of the founders of monasticism, Saint Benedict of Nursia. In this sense, every dwelling—as both noun and verb—is a *secum habitare*, a notion of being affected by oneself in and through the act of inhabiting a certain place in a certain way. People cannot *be* or *have* themselves, they can only *inhabit* themselves.

It is worth noting that Berthold Delbrück, the linguist who coined the term *Affiziertheit*, includes *mainomai*, 'to go mad', in his illustrative examples (alongside 'to rejoice' and 'to be ashamed').[4] To go mad (like to be born, Greek *gignomai*, Latin *nascor*) is a 'habitive' verb par excellence, and it is this third type of action that defines habit and its special continuity.

Towards the end of his essay 'Remarks on *Oedipus*', where the relationship between divinity and humanity is called into question, Hölderlin describes the resulting human condition as follows: *In der äußersten Grenze*

---

4 See Berthold Delbrück, *Vergleichende Syntax der indogermanischen Sprache*, VOL. 2 (Strasbourg: Trübner, 1897), p. 422.

*des Leidens bestehet nämlich nichts mehr, als die Bedingungen der Zeit oder des Raums*—'At the most extreme limit of suffering there remains indeed nothing more than the conditions of time and space.'[5] This is a clear reference to Kant's conception of time and space as conditions of sensibility, but it is mediated by a passage from Schiller's *Letters on Aesthetic Education*, which attempts to define a stage of the human spirit he terms 'mere determinability' (*bloße Bestimmbarkeit*). The nineteenth letter states:

> The condition of the human spirit before any determination, the one that is given it through impressions of the se nses, is an unlimited capacity for being determined. The boundlessness of space and time is presented to the human imagination for its free use [*zu freien Gebrauch*], and since *ex hypothesi* nothing in this wide realm of the possible is ordained, and consequently nothing is yet excluded, we may call this condition of indeterminability [*Bestimmungslosigkeit*] an empty infinity [*eine*

---

5 Friedrich Hölderlin, 'Übersetzungen' in *Sämtliche Werke*, VOL. 5 (Kleine Stuttgarter Ausgabe, F. Beissner ed.) (Stuttgart: Kohlhammer, 1954), p. 220.

*leere Unendlichkeit*], which is by no means to be confused with an infinite emptiness.[6]

According to Schiller, the passivity of this stage is to some extent active ('The finite spirit is that which only becomes active through passivity' [*durch Leiden*]).[7] Furthermore, in the subsequent letter, it is defined as a 'spontaneous passivity' (*Leiden mit Selbsttätigkeit*): 'In order, therefore, to exchange spontaneous passivity and inactive determination for an active one, he must be momentarily free from all determination and pass through a condition of mere determinability [*einen Zustand der bloßen Bestimmbarkeit*].'[8]

The dwelling or 'habitative' life that Hölderlin tries to conceive of and live is to be found, following Schiller, precisely at that 'extreme limit of suffering', where 'there remains indeed nothing more than the conditions of time and space', a 'mere determinability' quite similar to what Schiller's contemporary Maine

---

6 Friedrich Schiller, 'Über die ästhetische Erziehung des Menschen in einer Reihe von Briefen', in *Sämtliche Werke*, vol. 5 (Munich: Hanser, 1962), p. 626.

7 Schiller, 'Über die ästhetische Erziehung des Menschen', p. 627.

8 Schiller, 'Über die ästhetische Erziehung des Menschen', p. 632.

de Biran calls an *état purement affectif*. The latter's *Mémoire sur la décomposition de la pensée* defines this as 'a unique relationship of passivity' which, above and beyond all conscious perception, 'can constitute ... an impersonal mode of existence',[9] a state of pure *affectibilité* he nevertheless considers 'a positive and complete mode of existence'.[10] Habitative life is, then, a state of affect or 'affectibility' that remains such even when it receives affections; instead of transforming them into conscious perceptions, it allows them to pass into a superior coherence without ascribing them to an identifiable subject. Hence, for Hölderlin, the self (i.e. the I or ego) cannot take the form of an absolute subject that posits itself—as in the work of Fichte and early Schelling—but must instead assume the more fleeting and unappropriable form of a habit or habitual action.

The accounts of Hölderlin's friends and visitors repeatedly refer to the notion of *Zusammenhangslosigkeit*, an incoherence or disjointedness in his thought and speech. He utters single sentences that make sense on their own yet have no connection to

---

9 Maine de Biran, *Mémoire sur la décomposition de la pensée*, in *Oeuvres*, VOL. 3 (F. Azouvi ed.) (Paris: Vrin, 1988), p. 389.

10 Biran, *Mémoire sur la décomposition de la pensée*, p. 370.

subsequent ones. As Waiblinger writes in his biography: 'Hölderlin had become incapable of concentrating on a thought, clarifying it, elaborating on it, linking it to other analogous thoughts, and including it in a coherent string of sentences, even with less closely related thoughts.' The same can be said of his poetry from a certain point onwards: as both Jakobson and Adorno have pointed out—and as was already implicit in von Hellingrath's aforementioned concept of *harte Fügung*—Hölderlin's late work is distinguished by an extreme parataxis and the deliberate absence of any hypotactic coordination. Furthermore, Hamacher has commented on its parenthetic phrasing—whereby, in addition to pauses, sentences are embedded in one another.[11] One could say that this lack of connection gradually becomes a working principle of poetic composition. This is true of both the hymns—in which single, striking apophthegms follow one another without any apparent relationship—as well as the rhymed poems of his later years, in which scenes from the natural world follow one another in a continuous yet apparently incoherent manner.

---

11 Werner Hamacher, *Two Studies of Friedrich Hölderlin* (Peter Fenves and Julia Ng eds; Julia Ng and Anthony Curtis Adler trans) (Stanford, CA: Stanford University Press, 2020), p. 41.

A fragment from 1799—perhaps intended for *Iduna,* a magazine that remained unpublished—proves that Hölderlin had in fact already consciously worked towards going beyond a 'merely logical' connection between words and sentences. Just as word order can be inverted within a sentence, he writes,

> inversion of the sentences themselves will have an even broader and stronger effect. Certainly the logical arrangement [*logische Stellung*] of sentences—whereby the main clause [*Grund*] is followed by a becoming [*Werden*], the becoming is followed by an aim [*Ziel*], the aim is followed by an end [*Zweck*], and the subordinate clauses [*Nebensätze*] are always only linked to the main clause, to which they refer in the first place—can hardly ever be used by the poet.[12]

The overtly philosophical terminology (*Grund, Werden, Zweck*) suggests that the poetological principle being stated here is also a logical and ontological principle, as if Hölderlin were trying to articulate another—not strictly logical—way of connecting thoughts. In any case, two points are clear: first, a purely syntactic-grammatical conception of parataxis

---

12 Hölderlin, 'Der Tod des Empedokles', p. 243.

cannot sufficiently account for the complexity of the phenomenon; second, what is at issue for Hölderlin isn't merely an absence of coherence or connection (*Zusammenhangslosigkeit*), but rather a higher form of cohesiveness, which he calls 'infinite connection' (*unendlicher Zusammenhang*) or even 'infinite unity' (*unendliche Einheit*).

A reading of Hölderlin's lengthy, unfinished essay 'On the Operations of the Poetic Spirit' shows how he obsessively returns to this point: it is discussed as the relationship between 'harmonic unity' (*harmonische Einigkeit*) and 'harmonic alternation' (*harmonische Wechsel*)—i.e. between the unity and identity of the poetic spirit on the one hand, and the multiplicity of oppositions through which it is articulated, on the other. The poetic spirit risks losing its unity and totality in this split, turning into an empty infinity of isolated moments:

> Once it is so advanced, once its transactions
> lack neither harmonious unity nor significance
> and energy, neither harmonious spirit in gen-
> eral nor harmonious alternation, then it is
> necessary—if the unified [*das Einige*] (to the
> extent I that it can be considered by itself) shall
> not cancel itself as something undifferentiable

[*Ununterscheidbares*], and become an empty infinity [*leeren Unendlichkeit*], or if it shall not lose its identity in an alternation of opposites, however harmonious they may be, thus be no longer anything integral and unified [*Ganzes und Einiges*], but shall disintegrate into an infinity of isolated moments (a sequence of atoms, as it were)—I say: then it is necessary that the poetic spirit in its unity and harmonious progress also provide for itself an infinite perspective for its transaction, a unity wherein the harmonious progress and alternation everything move forward and backward and, through its sustained characteristic relation to that unity, not only gain objective coherence for the observer [but] also gain [a] felt and tangible coherence and identity [*Zusammenhang und Identität*] in the alternation of oppositions; and it is its last task, to have a thread, to have a recollection so that the spirit remain present to itself never in the individual moment and again in an individual moment, but continue in one moment as in another and in the different moods [*Stimmungen*], just as it is entirely present to itself in the infinite unity [*unendlichen*

*Einheit*], which is once the point of separation for the unified as such, but then again also point of union for the unified as the opposed, finally is also both at once [*beides zugleich*], so that what is harmoniously opposed within it is neither opposed as something unified nor unified as something opposed but as both in One, is felt as opposed in unified manner as inseparable and is invented as something felt.[13]

In this almost breathless passage, Hölderlin grapples with a rather lofty task—nothing less than identifying how two opposites (the unity and multiplicity of oppositions into which the poetic spirit seems to split) might coincide. This cannot be dialectically resolved through synthesis, following the Hegelian model, but rather is a question of how these two instances coincide while remaining inseparable, following Benjamin's dialectic at a standstill (*Stillstand*): 'Poetic individuality', Hölderlin concludes, 'is therefore never the mere opposition of what is unified, nor [is it] ever the mere relation [or] unification of the opposing and changing; what is opposed and unified is inseparable

---

13 Hölderlin, 'Der Tod des Empedokles', pp. 261–62; *Essays and Letters on Theory* (Thomas Pfau trans.) (Albany: State University of New York Press, 1988), pp. 70–1.

GIORGIO AGAMBEN

[*unzertrennlich*] within it.'[14] As in his essay *Urteil und Sein* (Judgment and Being), it is above all a matter of neutralizing the Fichtean reconciliation of opposites through reflection, and this is made clear a few lines later: '[I]f within it unity and opposition are inseparably linked and one, then it can appear to reflection neither as an opposable unity [*entgegensetzbares Einiges*] nor as a unifiable opposition [*vereinbares Entgegengesetzes*], [and] thus cannot appear at all or only in the character of a positive nothing, an infinite stagnation [*unendlichen Stillstands*].'[15]

That what is at issue here is another aspect of continuity and connection becomes evident in the expressions Hölderlin uses both in the aforementioned essay (i.e. *Zusammenhang und Identität, unendlich einiger und lebendiger Einheit*) as well as in others. In the essay 'On Religion', a *höherer und unendlicher Zusammenhang* ('higher and more infinite cohesion') is at issue, and in his Pindaric fragment *Das Unendliche* ('The Infinite'), we read that two concepts 'connect infinitely' (*unendlich . . . zusammehängen*) 'in a continuous relationship' (*durchgängiger Beziehung*).[16] It is noteworthy that

---

14 Hölderlin, 'Der Tod des Empedokles', p. 262.
15 Hölderlin, 'Der Tod des Empedokles', p. 263.
16 Hölderlin, 'Übersetzungen', p. 311.

308

Hölderlin uses the qualification 'more infinite' several times, as if paradoxically contrasting two forms of infinity, one 'alive', the other 'empty' (*leere Unendlichkeit*) and 'dead and deadly' (*tote und tötende Einheit*). By defining the empty infinity as made up of infinite isolated elements, similar to 'a sequence of atoms', and then contrasting this with another, 'complete' and 'unified' infinity, Hölderlin seems to anticipate Cantor's theorem. Noting that the continuum is uncountable—that real numbers are a larger infinity than integers—Cantor distinguishes between infinite and transfinite sets, and states that 'the cardinality of the continuum, which is the same as that of the power set of the integers, is strictly larger than the cardinality of the integers'. In the Hölderlinian continuum, as in Cantor's, the elements are so infinitely connected that it is impossible to insert another between them: separation and unity, opposition and identity perfectly coincide—that is, they fall together.

This uncountable continuity is what defines both Hölderlin's dwelling life and the exaggerated parataxis of his late poetry. There is no coordination between life's various moments, nor between the poet's disconnected thoughts and verses, because they are 'more infinitely connected'—not according to any 'logical arrangement', but rather in their being cohesively juxtaposed in a state of arrest. The 'but' (*aber*) that often marks this standstill in the poems isn't adversative, it doesn't indicate an opposition, which would just be yet another form of coordination: it merely marks an impasse between lines and thoughts, which follow one another without allowing any possibility of inserting logical coordination between one and the next. As von Hellingrath noted when speaking of a 'rigid construction', the decisive aspect here isn't the ordered semantic discourse of propositions, but rather the sentence or even the individual word in its asemantic isolation. And it is in light of this interrupted or stalled dialectic that the theory of caesura that Hölderlin develops in his essay 'Remarks on *Oedipus*' should be read. In the rhythmic sequence of representations that define the movement of the tragic word, Hölderlin writes, 'there becomes necessary *what in poetic meter is called cesura,* the pure word, the counter-rhythmic rupture; namely, in order to meet the onrushing change of representations at its highest point in such a manner that very soon there does not appear the change of representation but the representation itself.'[17] Thus the paratactic intention culminates in the caesura, and what surfaces in this anti-rhythmic interruption is not the semantic flow of representative discourse, but language itself. This

---

17 Hölderlin, 'Übersetzungen', p. 214.

is why Hölderlin makes the stretch of defining cesura, the interruption of discourse, as 'the pure word' (*das reine Wort*)—the eccentric place where what appears isn't intralinguisic discourse but language as such.

Precisely because, in a certain sense, the late poems are stalled blocks of language, they come to us in not just one but several versions. These multiples—as scholars have clearly understood, diplomatically reproducing all the manuscript drafts of given pieces instead of presenting a single critical text—are not various approaches to some ultimate form or meaning that just happens to have missed the mark. Rather, they are a poem's 'di-versions' from itself—a poem that can only exist in potentially infinite movement, diverging from itself and, at the same time, turning to itself. If the 'verse' of poetry is—etymologically speaking, from the Latin *versare*, 'to turn'—language that 'turns', and returns to itself by diverging from itself, then Hölderlin's late work pushes the 'versive' nature of poetic language to its extreme. This is true of the hymns, which must be read in all their almost simultaneously penned drafts, but it is also true of the poems from the tower. The latter are often variations on a theme the poet ironically proposed to his visitors— 'Shall I write about Greece, spring, or the spirit of the age?'—and thus understandably seem rather repetitive. In these poems, as in life, Hölderlin was attempting to capture the sense of habit; thus they are also, so to speak, 'inhabitant poems', 'dwelling poems'. This also explains the curious admonition in his 'Remarks on *Oedipus*', according to which: 'Modern poetry . . . lacks especially training and craftsmanship, namely, that its mode of operation can be calculated and taught and, once it has been learned, is always capable of being repeated reliably in practice.'[18]

This is the thorny context within which one must consider the many different names that, from a certain time onwards, Hölderlin used for himself: Scardanelli (Skartanelli), Killalusimeno, Scaliger Rosa, Salvator Rosa, Buarroti (Buonarroti), Rosetti. Various explanations have been proposed for the name Scardanelli, with which he signed his poems from 1837 or 1838 onwards, although none are entirely convincing. But we can be certain that Hölderlin used Scardanelli above all for his poetry: as C. T. Schwab recalls, when asked to sign Hölderlin under the poems he had given him, the irritated poet shouted, 'My name is Scardanelli' (or Skardanelli); and J. G. Fischer, who showed Hölderlin the second edition of his poems, was told: 'Yes, the poems are authentic, they are mine, but the name is wrong; I have never been called Hölderlin,

---

18 Hölderlin, 'Übersetzungen', p. 213.

I go by Scardanelli or Scarivari or Scaliger Rosa . . . '
(in a later version of this account—see the passage
quoted in the chronology for 1843—Fischer corrected
himself: 'I have never in my life been called Hölderlin,
I go by Scardanelli or Scaliger Rosa . . . '). But Gustav
Schlesier reported finding poems signed Scardanelli in
Hölderlin's family home as early as 1837: 'He got it
into his head that his name was no longer Hölderlin,
but Scartanelli or even Buarooti.'

As Jakobson noted, the name Scardanelli is a dim-
inutive, as is the name Hölderlin (from *Holder*, elder),
and both names contain nearly all the same letters, just
in a different order: *-lderlin* / *-rdanelli*. Sattler saw an
anagram of the Greek word *katharsis* in Skartanelli,
forgetting that—as Starobinski showed for the ana-
grams Saussure read in Saturnian verse—any name can
be read anagrammatically, especially if the anagram
isn't perfect. Michael Knaupp reads an anagram in
Scaliger Rosa that is more arbitrary still: *Sacrileg'ossa*
('Sacrilegious bones'), which he just as arbitrarily interprets as a confession that Hölderlin was responsible
for Susette Gontard's death.[19] Knaupp's subsequent
suggestion of a similarity between Scardanelli and the

---

19 Michael Knaupp, 'Scaliger Rosa', *Hölderlin Jahrbuch* 25
(1986–87): 266.

Greek verb *skardamysso* (to blink or wink) is rather more plausible, as it appears in Euripides' *Cyclops* (and Hölderlin's personal library included a copy of Euripides' works). Many other scholars have observed the similarity between Scardanelli and the name Girolamo Cardano; as for the name Scaliger, it may refer to Giulio Cesare Scaligero, a humanist and philologist whose work was certainly familiar to Hölderlin, especially since Scaligero wrote a famous critique of Cardano's book *De subtilitate* (*Exotericarum exercitationum liber XV De Subtilitate ad Hyeronymum Cardanum*, Frankfurt 1607; legend has it that Cardano died of a broken heart while reading Scaligero's book). But none of these or any other possible juxtaposition implies anything more than coincidence, just as it is entirely coincidental that, in 1831, a student named Frassinelli happened to be among Zimmer's boarders.

What is crucial, on the other hand, is that these apocryphal names come up whenever Hölderlin is forced to assert his authorship. Consider his supposed statement, 'Yes, the poems are authentic, they are mine, but the name is wrong . . . ' (and note that in his later correction, Fischer quotes the latter part of the phrase as 'but the title is wrong'), followed by not just one name but three different names. The identity of the author is not what is fragmented and altered here; he didn't say, 'I did not write them, but someone else did', which is the kind of claim frequently made by people diagnosed with schizophrenia. As Luigi Reitani rightly observed, this isn't a matter of Hölderlin assuming a new *identity*, consciously or unconsciously; the only thing in question is his *name*, which appears in various iterations, all curiously tied to a foreign, Italian name.[20] Aristotle's comparison of comic versus tragic names comes to mind—in *Poetics* (1451b, 19–20), he notes that comic poets, once they have constructed the story, introduce names at random, whereas tragedy usually repeats real, historical names. The names that appear in tragic works are usually unique and immutable, since they tend to express a predestined link between a character and their actions; the names in comedic works, on the other hand, are not linked to a character's destiny or defects, and are therefore random— they are also often just nicknames, rather than real, formal names. Furthermore, just as Hölderlin's late poems exist in multiple versions, without that fact casting any doubt upon their 'more infinite cohesion' or 'infinite unity', so too does his name.

---

20 Luigi Reitani (ed.), *Hölderlin. Tutte le opere* (VOL. 1: *Tutte le liriche*; VOL. 2: *Prose, teatro e lettere*) (Milan: Mondadori, 2001), p. 81.

*Anacoluthon*, a Greek term referring to logically incoherent phrasing, literally means 'not following', and denotes sentences that are 'without sequence' or 'disconnected'. In this sense, everything Hölderlin wrote while holed up in the tower is an anacoluthon. But Hölderlin augments this syntactic-grammatical disconnect with yet another one, which might best be considered a theatrical disconnect. In ancient Greek comedy (specifically Attic comedy), after the main actors left the stage, the chorus moved towards the proscenium and into the *logeion* (literally 'place of speech'), where they would take off their masks and speak directly to the audience. That moment was called *parekbasis* (literally 'next-door exit'), a phenomenon Friedrich Schlegel wrote about at length, which is often translated into English as 'digression' (following the Latin calque of the Greek term). Schlegel saw it as not only the most quintessential aspect of ancient comedy but also the hallmark of Romantic literature:

> In its form, ancient Athenian comedy is quite similar to tragedy. Like tragedy, it has a chorus, a dramatic-dialogical aspect, and monody. The only difference lies in the *parekbasis*, a speech in the middle of the play whereby the chorus directly addresses the audience in the name of the poet. Indeed, it was a complete interruption

and adjournment [*eine gänzliche Unterbrechung und Aufhebung*] of the play, in which . . . the greatest licentiousness reigned, and the chorus came out to the edge of the proscenium and said the crudest things to the audience. The term derives from this 'stepping out' (*ekbasis*).[21]

According to Schlegel, the *parekbasis* allows the writer to step outside the dialectic of thesis and antithesis, which will ultimately be recomposed into a reflexive synthesis, and ironically expose the two elements in all their irreconcilable separation. The work thus produced is not a form in and of itself, but rather a 'supreme anti-form or nature poem' (*die höchste Antiform oder Naturpoesie*).[22] The case could be made that Hölderlin made constant use of an extreme form of theatrical *parekbasis*. As a writer, he didn't attempt to establish a unified, composed notion of the poet; rather, he exposed it in all its constituent, comic divisions— the poet *as* split personality. Standing before his own private audience of visitors, he incessantly stepped into and back out of the role of the poet, to such an extent that it became impossible to decide whether he was in character or not during any given visit. This pushes

---

21 Schlegel, *Kritische Ausgabe,* VOL. 2, p. 88.
22 See Hamacher, *Two Studies of Friedrich Hölderlin,* p. 223.

Romantic irony to an extreme while simultaneously laying it to rest, such that we can never know exactly who it is that asks: 'Shall I write about Greece, spring, or the spirit of the age?'

The 'versive' gesture of the poem is also a turning away from the foreign towards the native (or national) (*vaterländischer Umkehr*), which was the core intention of Hölderlin's outermost thinking, evident in his letter to Böhlendorff as well as his essay 'Remarks on *Antigone*'. Since the 'original' can only appear in a state of weakness, it can only be achieved through a round-trip journey that must first have ventured out into the foreign. One can only turn towards the origin—one returns to it without ever having been there before. The free use of the proper is the most difficult thing because what we are born with is not something that can be possessed once and for all, as a given; it can only be experienced as weakness and deprivation. It necess-arily assumes the form of a habit, in the sense in which Aristotle defined it in a passage of *Metaphysics* that Hölderlin might well have known: as the *hexis*, from *echein*, 'to have'—literally the act or state of 'having', just as from 'to be' the word 'being' was formed, or, to give an example from Latin, the verb *esse* ('to be') led to the analogical formation *essentia* ('essence' and also 'being'). Aristotle used *hexis* first and foremost in relation to deprivation, as something that cannot under any circumstances be had ('it is impossible to have a "having" [*echein hexin*] in this sense; for there will be an infinite series if we can have the having of what we have'—*Metaphysics* 1022b, 25). In other words, possession of one's origin is possible only in the 'habitual' sense, and only through the dispossession of a habitation and a habit: it cannot be had, one can only become used to it, accustomed to it, habituated to it. To have a having is, in the final analysis, only a way or mode [*modo*] of being, a form of life.

In an exemplary book on Indo-European languages, Émile Benveniste distinguished between two ways of forming nouns that indicate an action: on the one hand, nouns expressing an attitude or possibility (ending in *-tu* in Indo-Iranian, *-tys* in Greek, and *-tus* in Latin) and, on the other hand, nouns expressing a performed action (*-ti* in Indo-Iranian, *-sis* in Greek, *-tio* in Latin). Thus, in Latin *actus* means the state or manner in which someone or something moves or can move, *actio* the concrete action; *ductus* the manner in which something is or can be led, *ductio* the action of pulling or leading; *gestus* a way of behaving, *gestio*, the performance of an action.[23] Similarly, the supine, which

---

23 Benveniste, *Noms d'agent et noms d'action en indoeuropéen*, pp. 97–98.

is formed by adding the -*tu* suffix, 'expresses potential: *cubitum ire*, "to go to sleep", does not indicate a concrete, completed action, but rather a possibility'.[24] The Aristotelian distinction between potential or possibility (*dynamis*) and concrete act (*energeia*) is easy to recognize in these examples, but further elaborating on Benveniste's considerations might help us gain a better understanding of the relationship between the two categories.

Take the Latin term *habitus*, for instance: as a noun ending in -*tus*, it expresses an attitude or a possibility—or, more precisely, the way in which a power or possibility is had; not its objective exercise or concrete practice (which would be *hexis* in Greek; the Latin *habitio* developed relatively late). It becomes clear why Aristotle, who tried to think through his idea using the term *hexis* (which, as a noun ending in -*sis*, expresses a performed action) as a middle ground between mere potential and concrete act, encountered a challenge that proved quite difficult to overcome. Potential, expressed in the way language presents it, isn't something *not real* that precedes the act in which it is realized: it is, on the contrary, the only way in

---

24 Benveniste, *Noms d'agent et noms d'action en indoeuropéen*, p. 100.

which we can have what we do. That is, we can 'have' actions insofar as we consider them real possibilities for us: the moment they are performed, these actions become so separated from their subjects that they must be ascribed or attributed (to their actors, or the people who carry them out—hence the notion of guilt, upon which both law and tragedy are based).

Custom or habit [*l'abito o l'abitudine*]—the inhabiting, dwelling life we are attempting to define—neutralize the *dynamis/energeia* opposition, rendering it inoperative. In keeping with a Hölderlinian penchant which should be familiar by now, they consider opposites in their inseparable coinciding.

In 1838, when Hölderlin was still living in his tower on the Neckar, the French philosopher Félix Ravaisson, who had studied with Schelling in Munich, wrote a treatise titled *De l'habitude* (Of Habit). In dizzying pages that gained the admiration of Bergson and Heidegger, 25-year-old Ravaisson approaches habit as one of life's ultimate secrets. He describes with meticulous precision the ways in which habit almost imperceptibly causes one's will to morph into inclination and instinct, in a progressive degradation of effort and intention that, just as in Hölderlin's work, is both passive and active: 'The law of habit can be explained only by the development of a Spontaneity that is at once active and passive, equally opposed to mechanical Fatality and to reflective Freedom.'[25] In the case of conscious reflection and will, which we generally consider higher-level human functions, the end is an idea that does not yet exist and must therefore be brought about through action or movement; in the case of habit, however, the end is confused with the very action or movement that would bring it about, hence the subject and object become indeterminate:

> The interval that the understanding represents between the movement and its goal gradually diminishes; the distinction is effaced; the end whose idea gave rise to the inclination comes closer to it, touches it and becomes fused with it. An immediate intelligence, in which nothing separates the subject and object of thought, gradually replaces the reflection that traverses and measures distances between contraries, the middle ground between opposing terms.[26]

A sort of 'dark intelligence'[27] is at work here, in which not only the real and the ideal coincide, but

---

25 Félix Ravaisson, *Of Habit* (Clare Carlisle and Mark Sinclair trans) (London and New York: Continuum, 2008), p. 55.

26 Ravaisson, *Of Habit*.

27 Ravaisson, *Of Habit*.

even one's individual will and nature tend to infinitely coincide: 'Habit is thus, so to speak, the infinitesimal *differential*, or, the dynamic *fluxion* from Will to Nature.'[28] As in Hölderlin's dwelling, inhabiting life, which abdicates both name and identity, 'the progression of habit leads consciousness, by an uninterrupted degradation, from will to instinct, and from the accomplished unity of the person to the extreme diffusion of impersonality'.[29]

The unprecedented culmination of Ravaisson's thesis—or, if you will, of his philosophical poem—is when habit turns out to provide the key to understanding the most basic functions of life:

> The most elementary mode of existence, with the most perfect organization, is like the final moment of habit, realized and substantiated in space in a physical form. The analogy of habit penetrates its secret and delivers its sense over to us. All the way down to the confused and multiple life of the zoophyte, down to plants, even down to crystals, it is thus possible to trace, in this light, the last rays of thought and activity as they are dispersed and dissolved

---

28 Ravaisson, *Of Habit*, p. 59.
29 Ravaisson, *Of Habit*, p. 65.

without yet being extinguished, far from any possible reflection, in the vague desires of the most obscure instincts. The whole series of beings is therefore only the continuous progression of the successive powers of one and the same principle, powers enveloping one another in the hierarchy of the forms of life, powers which develop in the opposite direction within the progression of habit. The lower limit is necessity—Destiny, as might be said, but in the spontaneity of Nature; the higher limit is the Freedom of the understanding. Habit descends from the one to the other; it brings these contraries together, and in doing so reveals their intimate essence and their necessary connection.[30]

Seen from this perspective, even love—whereby individual will gives way to nature and desire—is akin to habit, which becomes something like the ultimate basis of life, its deepest core, which we cannot grasp rationally: 'It is God within us, God hidden solely by being so far within us in this intimate source of ourselves, to whose depths we do not descend.'[31]

---

30 Ravaisson, *Of Habit*, p. 67.
31 Ravaisson, *Of Habit*, p. 71.

Ultimately, in the book's supreme ontological conclusion, habit is identified as the very essence of substance according to Spinoza: 'Finally, the disposition of
which habit consists, and the principle engendering it,
are one and the same thing: this is the primordial law
and the most general form of being, the tendency to
persevere in the very actuality that constitutes being.'[32]
The *conatus*, the tension through which each thing
perseveres in its being, cannot be an act of the will, nor
can it be an arbitrary decision: it can only be a habit, a
dwelling life.

We can now try to further clarify the connection
between the habitual, the (in)habitant (or dwelling)
and the 'habitive' [*l'abituale, l'abitante e l'abitivo*] in
Hölderlin's thought. Hölderlin's life of dwelling or
inhabitant life is 'habitive' because it is not just a series
of voluntary, attributable actions but rather is a form
of life, a being that is affected, at every single moment,
by its own habits. This is why Hölderlin, at a certain
point, willingly accepts the diagnosis of his madness—
just as Walser did a century later. And he not only keeps
it up for the rest of his life, he even seems intentionally
to play it up in front of visitors. Someone deemed mad
is, by definition, devoid of any legal capacity, and is

---

32 Ravaisson, *Of Habit*, p. 77.

therefore not held responsible for their actions. One after the other, Burk, Zeller and Essig assume the role of *curator furiosi*, negotiating on Hölderlin's behalf with Zimmer and his daughter, with the poet's relatives and with the publisher, thereby controlling the economic conditions and details of Hölderlin's everyday existence. It would seem, then, impossible to imagine anything more private than his existence. And yet the obstinacy with which he insists on being addressed as 'Herr Librarian' and granting his visitors titles that belong almost exclusively to the public sphere ('Your Majesty', 'Mister Baron, sir', 'Your Holiness') introduces a claim to publicness in this otherwise reclusive life. Hölderlin's dwelling life neutralizes the opposition between public and private, making them coincide, without synthesis, in a stalled position, a stalemate. In this sense, his 'inhabiting life', neither private nor public, is perhaps his truest political and philosophical legacy. In this aspect, too, he is close to us and our present-day society—as we, too, no longer distinguish between the two spheres. His life prophesied something that no one in his era could conceive of without verging on madness.

Such a life is not tragic if tragedy, as defined in Aristotle's *Poetics*, implies above all the characteristics of a person's actions ('tragedy is the imitation not of people but of action . . . people do not act in order to imitate characters, they assume characters through actions', 1450a, 16–22). If tragedy is the sphere of attributable action, comedy, by contrast, is a sphere in which people seem to lay aside all responsibility for their actions. Comic actors imitate their character, thereby abdicating all responsibility for their actions, which are ultimately just gags and senseless gestures, like the ceremonial titles Hölderlin assigns his visitors in the tower. But if Hölderlin could be said to have abandoned the tragic paradigm at some point, it doesn't mean that he simply chose comedy instead. Rather, he once again neutralized the opposition between tragic and comic, heading in the direction of something neither tragic nor comic, for which we lack a proper term. Humankind's habitation on earth is neither a tragedy nor a comedy, it is a simple, everyday, trite act of dwelling, an anonymous and impersonal form of life—it can speak and make gestures, but neither discourse nor action can be attributed to it.

In this sense, Hölderlin's life constitutes its own paradigm and, in comparison, the categorical oppositions that define our culture come up short: active-passive, comic/tragic, public/private, reason/ madness, mere possibility/actual act, sensible/nonsense, united/ separate. Precisely because this life dwells on an undecidable threshold, it isn't easy to compete with it, or to try to derive a model from it. This is all the more true since, evidently, success/failure is the very first opposition to fall away—as if failure were taken for granted while at the same time, almost like the absence of the gods, it is transformed into assistance, into a resource. What Hölderlin teaches us is that, for whatever purpose we might have been created, we certainly weren't created for success; the fate assigned to us is failure—in every art, in every realm of study, and above all in the sheer art of living. And yet this very failure— if we manage to seize it—is the absolute best we can do, just as Hölderlin's apparent defeat entirely deposes Goethe's success, stripping it of all legitimacy.

Ultimately, for Hölderlin, a life of dwelling is a poetic life, since *dichterisch, wohnet der Mensch auf dieser Erde,* 'poetically man dwells on this earth'. The German verb *dichten* etymologically derives from the Latin *dictare,* 'to dictate'; because classical authors used to dictate their compositions to scribes, the term gradually assumed the meaning of *poetare,* 'to compose literary works'. A poetic life, a life that dwells poetically, is a life lived according to a dictate—in other words, in a way that cannot be decided or mastered according to habit or custom, a 'having' that we can never have, but only inhabit.

For almost a year now I've been living with Hölderlin, day in and day out—over recent months in an isolation I never could've imagined I'd find myself. As I take my leave of him now, his madness strikes me as rather innocent compared with the madness into which an entire society has fallen without even realizing it. If I try to spell out the political lesson I seem to have gleaned from the dwelling life of the poet in his tower on the Neckar, for the time being I can perhaps 'only babble and babble'. There are no readers. There are only words with no addressee. The question 'what does it mean to dwell poetically?' still awaits an answer. *Pallaksh. Pallaksh.*

**17.** Portrait of Hölderlin, etching after an original charcoal drawing by J. G. Schreiner (1826), *circa* 1890.

# CATALOGUE OF BOOKS AT HÖLDERLIN'S HOUSE IN NÜRTINGEN

## 1. GREEK AND LATIN TEXTS

Aeschylus

> *Aeschyli Prometheus vinctus* (Halae Schulz ed.) [*Prometheus Bound*].

Aristotle

> *Aristotelis Organon,* Francofurti, MDXCVIII [Organon].
> *Aristotelis de Moribus,* 10 VOLS ['On Death'].
> *Aristotelis Technae Rhetoricae,* Biblia V [Rhetoric].

Aurelius, Marcus

> *Marci Antonini Philosophi Commentarii,* Lipsiae [*The Meditations*].

Balde, Jakob

> *Jacobi Balde Satyrica,* 1660 [Selected satires]

Barclay, John

> *Joh. Barclaii Argenis,* Amsterdolami, 1671 [*Argenis*].

Caesar

> *Caesaris Commentarii,* Antverpiae, 1585 [Caesar's commentaries].

Cicero

  *M. Tullii Ciceronis De finibus bonorum et malorum* [*On the
  Ends of Good and Evil*].

  *M. Tullii Ciceronis Opera omnia*, Lugduni, MDLXXXVIII
  [Complete works].

Euripides

  *Euripides*, 2 vols.

  *Euripidis Resos* [*Rhesus*].

Hesiod

  *Hesiodus*, 2 vols.

Homer

  *Homeri opera, graece et latine expressa*, Basileae,
    MDCCLXXIX.

  *Tomus I, continens Iliadem* [*Illiad*].

  *Tomus II, Odysseam* [*Odyssey*].

  *Homeri Ilias graece et latine*, Hauniae et Lipsiae, 1786 [*Illiad*].

Justin

  *Trogus Justinu*, Vratislaviae MDCLX [Pompeius Trogus'
    *Philippic Histories*].

  *Justini Historiae ad modum Minellii, in duplo* [Pompeius
    Trogus' *Philippic Histories*, edited by Johannes
    Minellus].

Lucan

  *M. Annaei Lucani de bello civili*, 10 VOLS [*Pharsalia* ('On the
    Civil War')].

Palaephatus

> *Palaephatus* [Likely *Peri Apiston*, 'On Incredible Things'].

Palingenius [Pier Angelo Manzolli]

> *Marcelli Palingenii Zodiacus Vitae*, Roterodami, 1648 ['The Zodiac of Life'].

Pindar

> *Pyndari Olympia, Pythia, Nemea, Isthmia*, 1560 [*Victory Odes: Olympian, Pythian, Nemean, Isthmian*].

Plato

> *Platonis Opera*, 12 VOLS.
>
> *Platonis Dialogorum Argomenta, 1 Tomus* [*Dialogues*].

Plutarch

> *Plutarchi opera*, Tubingae, MDCCXCIII, 4 VOLS [Selected works].
>
> *Plutarchs Werke, griechisch* [Selected works, in Greek].

Sophocles

> *Sophoclis Tragoediae septem*, Francofurti, 1555 [*Seven Tragedies*].

Tacitus

> *Taciti Opera* 1595 [Selected works].

Terence

> *Publii Terentii Aphri Comoediae sex. T. II*, Biponti, 1780 [Six comedies].

Theocritus

> *Theochriti Idyllia cum Scholis Selectis*, Gothae, 1782 [*Bucolics* and other selected works].

Virgil

*Virgilii Maronis Opera cum annotationibus Minellii* [Selected works, annotated by Johannes Minellus].

Volborth, J. C. [Johan Karl] (ed.)

*Chestomathia tragica Greaeco-latina*, Goettingae, 1776 [A compendium of Greek tragedies, including work by Aeschylus, Sophocles, Euripides and Seneca].

## 2. GERMAN POETRY

Justi, Johann Heinrich Gottlob von

Des Herrn von Justi, *Scherzhafte und Satyrische Schriften*, 3 VOLS, Berlin, 1765 [Selected satires].

Klopstock, Friedrich Gottlieb

*Klopstocks Gelehrten Bibliothek*, Part 1, Hamburg, 1774 [Selected works].

*Klopstocks Hermanns Schlacht*, Reutlingen, 1777 ['Hermann's Battle'].

*Klopstocks Geistliche Lieder*, Reutlingen, 1780 [*Odes*].

*Klopstocks Messias*, 3 VOLS, Reutlingen, 1782 [*The Messiah*].

Rüdiger, Johann Christian (ed.)

*Taschenbuch für Freunde des Gesanges*, Stuttgart, 1795 [Magazine with music and lyrics].

Weiße, Christian Felix

*Weißes Trauerspiele*, 3 VOLS, Reutlingen, 1776 [Tragedies].

Weppen, Johann August

*Gedichte*, Carlsruhe, 1783 [Poetry].

Wieland, Christoph Martin

> *Der neue Amadis. Ein comisches Gedicht in 18 Gesängen I,* Carlsruhe, 1777 [A romantic comedy in verse].
>
> *Musarion. Ein Gedicht,* Reutlingen 1780 [Poetry].

Zachariä, Justus Friedrich Wilhelm

> *Poetische Schriften von Zachariä,* 1, 3, and 4, Reutlingen 1778 [Poetry collection].

## 3. THEOLOGY

> *Novum Testamentum graecum et latinum,* Lipsiae 1575 [New Testament in Greek and Latin].
>
> *Novum Testamentum graecum,* 1734 [New Testament in Greek].
>
> *Hebräischer Psalter,* 1556 [Psalms in Hebrew].
>
> *Chaldaismi Biblici Fundamenta p.p.,* Tubingae, 1770 ['Chaldean' Bible, in Biblical Aramaic].
>
> *Compendium Theologiae Dogmaticae,* Stuttgardiae, 1782 [Compendium of dogmatic theology].
>
> *Joh. Gerh. Schellers Anleitung p.p.,* Halle 1783 [Introduction to Greek and Hebrew, by Immanuel Johann Gerhard Scheller].
>
> *D. Jo. Reinhardts Christliche Moral* [Christian morals].
>
> *Zweiter Theil von Predigten über die Sonntäglichen Episteln* [Sermons on the Epistles].

## 4. PHILOSOPHY

Anonymous

> *Das Petitionrecht der Wirtembergischen Landstände*, 1797 [On the right of petition of the estates of Württemberg].

Anonymous [probably Johann Christoph Knaus]

> *Compendium Logicae*, Stuttgardiae, 1751 [Compendium of logic].

Bacon, Francis

> Franc. Baco de Verulamio, *Liber de sapientia veterum* [*The Wisdom of the Ancients*].

Eberhard, Johann Augustus

> Joh. August Eberhard, *Neue Apologie des Sokrates*, 2 VOLS, Frankfurt and Leipzig, 1787 ['A New Apology for Socrates'].

> [J.]A. Eberhard, *Philosophische Magazin*, no. 1, Halle, 1788 [Philosophical magazine edited by Eberhard].

Fichte, Johann Gottlieb

> Fichte, *Grundlage des Naturrechts*, Jena, 1796 [*Foundations of Natural Right*].

Hume, David

> D. Hume, *Untersuchung über den menschlichen Verstand*, Jena, 1793 [*An Enquiry Concerning Human Understanding*].

Jacobi, Friedrich Heinrich

> F. H. Jacobi, *Über die Lehre des Spinoza in Briefen an M. Mendelsohn*, Breslau, 1789 [Letters on Spinoza].

Kant, Immanuel

> Im. Kant, *Critik der reinen Vernunft*, Riga, 1790 [*Critique of Pure Reason*].

> Im. Kant, *Critik der Urtheilskraft*, Frankfurt und Leipzig, 1792 [*Critique of Judgment*].

Mauchart, Immanuel David

> J. D. Mauchart, *Allgemeines Repertorium für empirische Psychologie etc.*, 2 VOLS, Nürnberg, 1792 [General reference for empirical psychology].

Schelling, Friedrich Wilhelm Joseph

> F. W. J. Schelling, *Ich als Prinzip der Philosophie*, 2 VOLS, Tübingen, 1795 [*On the I as a Principle of Philosophy*].

> F. W. J. Schelling, *Ideen zu einer Philosophie der Natur*, Leipzig, 1797 [*Ideas Concerning a Philosophy of Nature*].

Schleiermacher, Friedrich

> Schleiermacher, *Uber die Religion. Reden an die Gebildeten unter ihren Verächtern*, Berlin, 1799 [*On Religion: Speeches to its Cultured Despisers*].

## 5. LINGUISTICS, DICTIONARIES, GRAMMAR BOOKS

Danz, Johann Andreas

> *Danzii Compendium Grammaticae ebraeo-chaldaicae, Editio sexta*, Jenae [Hebrew–Aramaic grammar].

Ernesti, Johann August

> Jo. Augusti Ernesti, *Clavis Ciceroniana*, Halae MDCCLXVIIII [Cicero].

Eschenburg, Johann Joachim

Eschenburg, *Handbuch der klassichen Literatur*, Berlin and Stettin, 1801 [Handbook of classical literature].

Estienne, Charles (Carolus Stephanus)

*Dictionarium Historicum ac poëticum*, MDCXV [Encyclopaedia].

Garth, Balthasar

*Garthurthius olim bilinguis jam trilinguis sive Lexicon Latino-Germanico-Graecum*, Norimbergae, 1658 [Trilingual Latin–German–Greek dictionary].

Gedike, Friedrich

Gedike, *Pindars Olympische Siegeshymnen*, 1777 [German translation of Pindar's *Olympian Odes*].

Ramsler, Johann Friedrich

*Ramslers Griechische Grammatik*, Stuttgart, 1767 [Greek grammar].

Schneider, Johann Gottlob

J. G. Schneider, *Versuch über Pindars Leben und Schriften*, Strasburg, 1774 [*On Pindar's Life and Work*].

Veneroni, Giovanni

*Dictionarium Caesareum, in quo quattuor principaliores Linguae Europae explicantur* [Quadrilingual Italian–French–German–Latin dictionary].

Vollbeding, Johann Christoph

*Griechisch-Deutsches Handwörterbuch zum Schulgebrauch*, Leipzig bei E. B. Schwickert, 1784 [Greek–German dictionary; with 1788 supplement].

# BIBLIOGRAPHY

For works cited in the chronicle of Hölderlin's life, see *A Note to the Reader*. All other references are listed here. Where available, details for English-language editions have been added by the translator.

BARWICK, Karl (ed.). *Flavii Sosipatri Charisii Artis grammaticae libri V.* Leipzig: Teubner, 1925.

BENJAMIN, Walter. 'Die Aufgabe des Übersetzers', in *Gesammelte Schriften* IV, 1. Frankfurt am Main: Suhrkamp, 1972. ['The Task of the Translator' (Harry Zohn trans.), in Rainer Schulte and John Biguenet (eds), *Theories of Translation: An Anthology of Essays from Dryden to Derrida.* Chicago: University of Chicago Press, 1992, pp. 71–82.]

——. *The Storyteller Essays* (Samuel Titan ed. and introd.; Tess Lewis trans.). New York: New York Review Books, 2019.

BENVENISTE, Émile. 'Supinum'. *Revue philologique* 58 (1932): 136–37.

——. *Noms d'agent et noms d'action en indoeuropéen.* Paris: Maisonneuve, 1948.

BERTAUX, Pierre. *Friedrich Hölderlin.* Frankfurt am Main: Suhrkamp, 2000.

BINDER, Wolfgang. *Hölderlin und Sophokles.* Tübingen: Hölderlinturm, 1992.

GIORGIO AGAMBEN

CARCHIA, Gianni. *Orfismo e tragedia*, NEW EDN. Macerata: Quodlibet, 2019.

CHRISTEN, Felix. *Eine andere Sprache*. Schupfart: Engeler, 2007.

BIRAN, Maine de. 'Mémoire sur la décomposition de la pensée', in *Oeuvres*, VOL. 3 (F. Azouvi ed.). Paris: Vrin, 1988.

DELBRÜCK, Berthold. *Vergleichende Syntax der indogermanischen Sprache*, VOL. 2. Strasbourg: Trübner, 1897.

FRANZ, Michael. '1806', in *Le pauvre Holterling. Blätter zur Frankfurter Ausgabe*. Frankfurt am Main: Rote Stern, 1983.

HAMACHER, Werner. *Entferntes Verstehen*. Frankfurt am Main: Suhrkamp, 1998.

———. *Two Studies of Friedrich Hölderlin* (Peter Fenves and Julia Ng ed.; Julia Ng and Anthony Curtis Adler trans). Stanford, CA: Stanford University Press, 2020.

HARTMANN, Moritz. 'Eine Vermuthung', in *Freya, Illustrierte Familien-Blätter* 1 (1861).

HEGEL, G. W. F. *Aesthetics: Lectures on Fine Art* (T. M. Knox trans.). Oxford: Clarendon Press, 1975.

HEGEL, Hannelore. *Isaac von Sinclair. Zwischen Fichte, Hölderlin und Hegel*. Frankfurt am Main: Klostermann, 1971.

HELLINGRATH, Norbert von. 'Hölderlins Wahnsinn', in *Zwei Vorträge. Hölderlin und die Deutschen; Hölderlins Wahnsinn*. Munich: Bruckmann, 1922, pp. 49–85.

HÖLDERLIN, Friedrich. 'Der Tod des Empedokles. Aufsätze', in *Sämtliche Werke*, VOL. 4 (Kleine Stuttgarter Ausgabe, F. Beissner ed.). Stuttgart: Kohlhammer, 1962. [*The Death of Empedocles* (David Farrell Krell trans.). Albany: SUNY Press, 2008].

——. *Essays and Letters* (Jeremy Adler and Charlie Louth eds and trans). London: Penguin Classics, 2009.

——. *Essays and Letters on Theory* (Thomas Pfau trans.). Albany: State University of New York Press, 1988.

——. 'Übersetzungen', in *Sämtliche Werke*, VOL. 5 (Kleine Stuttgarter Ausgabe, F. Beissner ed.). Stuttgart: Kohlhammer, 1954.

KNAUPP, Michael. 'Scaliger Rosa', *Hölderlin Jahrbuch* 25 (1986–87): 263–72.

KRAFT, Stephan. *Zum Ende der Komödie. Eine Theoriengeschichte des Happyends.* Göttingen: Wallstein, 2012.

LEOPARDI, Giacomo. *Canti* (Jonathan Galassi ed. and trans.). New York: Farrar, Straus and Giroux, 2012.

PORTERA, Mariagrazia. *Poesia vivente. Una lettura di Hölderlin.* Palermo: Aesthetica Preprint Supplementa, 2010.

RAVAISSON, Félix. *De l'Habitude. Metaphysique et morale.* Paris: Presses Universitaires de France, 1999 [*Of Habit* (Clare Carlisle and Mark Sinclair trans). London and New York: Continuum, 2008].

REITANI, Luigi (ed.). *Hölderlin. Tutte le opera*; VOL. 1: *Tutte le liriche*; VOL. 2: *Prose, teatro e lettere.* Milan: Mondadori, 2001.

SCHADEWALDT, Wolfgang. 'Hölderlins Übersetzung des Sophokles', in *Über Hölderlin.* Frankfurt am Main: Insel, 1970.

SCHILLER, Friedrich. 'Über naive und sentimentale Dichtung', in *Sämtliche Werke*, VOL. 5. Munich: Hanser, 1962. [*Two Essays: 'Naive and Sentimental Poetry' & 'On The Sublime'* (Julius A. Elias trans.). New York: Frederick Ungar, 1979].

———. 'Über die ästhetische Erziehung des Menschen in einer Reihe von Briefen', in *Sämtliche Werke*, VOL. 5. Munich: Hanser, 1962. [*On the Aesthetic Education of Man* (Keith Tribe trans.). New York: Penguin Classics, 2016].

SCHLEGEL, Friedrich. *Kritische Ausgabe*, VOL. 2: *Charakteristiken und Kritiken*. Munich, Paderborn and Vienna: Schöningh, 1967.

———. *Kritische* Ausgabe VOL. 9, *Wissenschaft der europäischen Literatur*. Munich, Paderborn and Vienna: Schöningh, 1975.

SCHMIDT, Jochen (ed.). *Friedrich Hölderlin: Sämtliche Werke und Briefe*, VOL. 2. Frankfurt am Main: Deutscher Klassiker, 1990.

SCHWAB, C. T. 'Hölderlins Leben', in *F.H'.s Sämtliche Werke*. Stuttgart and Tübingen, 1846.

SEIBT, Gustav. *Anonimo romano. Scrivere la storia alle soglie del Rinascimento*. Rome: Viella, 2000.

STAIGER, Emil. *Grundbegriffe der Poetik*. Zurich: Atlantis Verlag, 1946.

THEUNISSEN, Michael. *Pindar. Menschenlos und Wende der Zeit*. Munich: C.H. Beck, 2000.

VALLÉE, Gérard (ed.). *The Spinoza Conversations Between Lessing and Jacobi: Text with Excerpts from Ensuing Controversy*. Lanham, MD: University Press of America, 1988.

VENUTI, Lawrence. *The Translator's Invisibility: A History of Translation*. London and New York: Routledge, 1995.

WAIBLINGER, Wilhelm. *Friedrich Hölderlins Leben, Dichtung und Wahnsinn*. Leipzig: Brockhaus, 1831. Reissued in D. E.

Sattler (ed.), *Friedrich Hölderlin: Sämtliche Werke, Kritische Textausgabe*, VOL. 9. Darmstadt: Luchterhand, 1984. [*Friedrich Hölderlin's Life, Poetry and Madness* (Will Stone trans.). London: Hesperus, 2018.]

**NB:** The ongoing pandemic—in which supermarkets remain open but libraries are closed—has made it impossible to conduct library research; hence these entries provide all available bibliographic details, albeit not in complete form. Regrettably, this list of works cited—especially sources for the illustrations—remains incomplete.

# INDEX OF NAMES

Adorno, Theodor, 303

Alexander I of Russia, 102

Aristotle, 315, 318, 320, 326, 331

Arnim, Achim von, 148–51, 199, 217, 269

Arnim, Bettina von, 244, 247

Auberlen, professor, 265, 281–82

Auguste of Hesse-Homburg, Landgravine, 68, 208

Autenrieth (Autenried), Johann Heinrich Ferdinand, 30, 85, 91, 93, 95, 99, 101, 105

Baz, Christian, Burgomaster of Ludwigsburg, 62

Beck, Adolph, 101

Becker, councillor, 104

Beissner, Friedrich, 45

Benedict of Nursia, Saint, 299

Benjamin, Walter, 5–6, 8, 31, 36, 39

Benveniste, Émile, 297, 319–20

Bergson, Henri, 321

Bertaux, Pierre, 27, 30, 65, 69

Blanchot, Maurice, 72

Blankenstein, Alexander, 62–64

Böhlendorff, Casimir Ulrich, 23, 37, 51, 55, 144, 318

Bonaparte, Joseph, 80, 110

Börne, Karl Ludwig, 245

Brandauer, 286

Brentano, Clemens, 58, 59, 126, 145, 148, 150, 152

Breunlin, Heinrike, 200–07, 225, 283

Brissot, Jacques Pierre, 65

Bürger, Gottfried August, 181

Burk, Israel Gottfried, 199–201, 203, 211–12, 215–18, 223, 225–28, 235, 237, 240–41, 244, 264, 326

Calame, watchmaker, 61, 67

Cantor, Georg, 309

Carchia, Gianni, 41, 69

Cardano, Girolamo, 314

Charisius, 297–98

Carrière, Moriz, 269

Chasles, Philarète, 246

Cicero, Marcus Tullius, 34

Conz (Konz), Karl Philipp, 121, 123, 133, 163–65, 182, 184

Cotta, Johann Friedrich, 88, 94, 115, 125, 145, 159, 161, 164, 167–73, 195, 217, 257, 260, 269, 276, 281

Cramer (Kramer), Karl, 104, 181, 232

Cronegk (Kronegk), Johann Friedrich Freiherr von, 211, 232

Czolbe, Heinrich, 275

Daru, Pierre, 112

De La Motte Fouqué, Friedrich, 131, 141, 169

Delbrück, Berthold, 299

Denon, Vivant, 92

Denzel, Bernhard Gottlieb, 170

Diefenbach, Albert, 230

Dienst, Heinrich von, 159, 160–61, 163, 168–70, 172

Döring, Julius, 244

Eichhorn, Johann Gottfried, 233

Empedocles, 53–55, 123, 197, 218

Eser, Friedrich, 187

Essig, guardian, 278, 283, 326

Esslingen, Günther von, 226

Esslinger, Gottlieb, 202, 206

Euripides, 284, 314

Fernow, Karl Ludwig, 94, 100

Feucht, Philipp, 201, 248, 278

Fichte, Johann Gottlieb, 45–50, 82–84, 302, 308

Fischer, Johann Georg, 265, 281, 286, 312–14

Franz, Michael, 89

Frassinelli, student, 314

Frederick V, Landgrave of Hesse-Homburg, 22

Frederick William II, King of Prussia, 102

Frederick William III, King of Prussia, 84

Genast, Eduard, 116

Gensler, Johann, 84

Gerning, Johann Isaak, 61–62, 67–68

Gessner, Salomon, 51

Gfrörer, Louise, 242

Gleim, Johann Wilhelm Ludwig, 211, 232

Gmelin, Ferdinand Gottlob von, 136, 261, 268–69, 290, 292

Gogol, Nikolai Vasilyevich, 30

Gok (also Gock), Ida, 195,

Gok (also Gock), Johanna Christiana, 199

Gok (also Gock), Karl, 189, 191, 195, 200, 203, 257, 278, 284, 290, 292, 298,

Gontard, Susette, 21, 22, 69, 313

Gregory I, Pope (Saint Gregory the Great), 299

Günther, senior consistory advisor, 92, 226

Haberle, doctor, 100

Habermas, student, 271

Hagedorn, Friedrich von, 251

Haide, Friedrich, 100

Hamacher, Werner, 303

Hartlaub, Wilhelm, 283

Hartmann, Moritz, 17, 22

Haug, Friedrich, 159, 162, 174–77, 182, 186

Hebel, Johann Peter, 8

Hegel, Georg Wilhelm Friedrich, 25, 50–51, 69, 74, 80, 88, 100, 107, 127, 134, 208, 236–37, 251, 278, 307

Heidegger, Martin, 72, 296, 321

Hellingrath, Norbert von, 22, 35–36, 303, 310

Hensel, Luise, 152

Herwegh, Georg, 244

Hesse-Darmstadt, Caroline of, 85

Hinzenstern, Herr von, 124

Hoffmann, tailor, 244

Homer, 133, 216

Horace (Quintus Horatius Flaccus), 86

Huber, printmaker, 124

Humboldt, Friedrich Heinrich von, 52

Jakobson, Roman, 303, 313

Jean Paul (Johann Paul Friedrich Richter), 68

Kalb, Charlotte von, 68

Kant, Immanuel, 70, 300

Keller, Adelbert, 279

Keller, Louise, 270–71

Kerner, Justinus, 95, 97, 101, 103, 107, 115, 121, 126, 131, 141, 155, 159, 162–71, 173, 197, 255

Kirchner, Werner, 87, 89

Kleist, Heinrich von, 102, 104, 181, 219–20

Klopstock, Friedrich Gottlieb, 180, 211, 216, 232, 251

Knaupp, Michael, 313

Knebel, Karl Ludwig von, 100

Konz (Conz), Karl Philipp, 121, 123, 133, 163–65, 182, 184

Kosegarten, Ludwig Gotthard, 181

Köstlin, Heinrich, 126

Kramer (Cramer), Karl, 181

Kühne, Gustav, 237–38

Künzel, Carl, 227

Kutuzov, Mikhail Illarionovich, 78

Landauer, Christian, 25

Lattner, saddler, 67

Lebret, chancellor, 221

Lebret, Elise, 207

Lebret, Johann Paul Friedrich, 207

Lenau, Nikolaus, 271

Lerebours, Favorin, 44

Lessing, Gotthold Ephraim, 86, 183n1

Lohbauer, Rudolf, 189

Louise of Hesse-Darmstadt, 90

Luden, Heinrich, 86

Mahlmann, August, 121, 125

Mährlen, Johannes, 207, 212

Maier (Mair), Friederike, 216, 221, 235

Maine de Biran (Marie-François-Pierre Gonthier de Biran), 301–02

Mäken, Frau, 172

Manfredini, Luigi, 100

Marat, Jean-Paul, 65

Marie Louise, Duchess of Parma, 124

Maria Anna of Hesse-Homburg, 68, 85, 208

Maria Theresa of Habsburg, Empress, 9

Mariotte, Edme, 122

Marx, Karl, 284

Matthisson (Matthison), Friedrich von, 15, 181, 233, 256

Mayer, August, 128, 132

Mayer, Karl, 159

Meyer, Daniel Christoph, 15, 94, 100, 110, 124

Miollis, Sextius Alexandre François de, 110

Mohrenheim, Arthur Pavlovich von, 102

Mörike, Eduard, 189–90, 196, 212, 235–36, 283

Müller, cobbler, 216, 226

Müller, Georg Friedrich Karl, 66

Müller, von, ambassador, 116

Müllner, Adolf, 193

Murat, Joachim, 110, 112

Napoleon I Bonaparte, Emperor, 63, 78, 80, 82, 84, 88, 90, 92, 98, 100, 102, 106, 110, 112, 113, 120, 124

Nast, Emanuel, 203

Nathusius, Marie, 263

Neuffer, Christian Ludwig, 41, 73, 159, 182, 206, 242

Newton, Isaac, 100, 122

Niethammer, Friedrich Immanuel, 88, 233

Nietzsche, Friedrich, 72

Niendorf, Emma (Emma von Suckow), 190

Novalis (Georg Philipp Friedrich Freiherr von Hardenberg), 269


Orsini, Bertollo, 7


Paisiello, Giovanni, 234

Pappenheim, Herr von, 86

Paristeer, Herr von, 195

Pfisterer, tailor, 220

Phocas, 298

Pindar, 34, 68, 179, 284, 308

Pius VII (Barnaba Niccolò Maria Luigi Chiaramonti), Pope, 80, 110

Portius, Simon, 116

Proek, Frau von, 91

Ramler, Karl Wilhelm, 62

Rapp, doctor, 292

Ravaisson, Félix, 321–25

Reitani, Luigi, 315

Ridel, councillor, 94

Riemer, Friedrich Wilhelm, 80, 88, 92

Rosenkranz, Karl, 278

Runge, Arnold, 284

Runge, Otto, 126


Sartorius, Georg Friedrich, 114, 122

Saussure, Ferdinand de, 313

Savary, Anne Jean Marie René, 116

Savigny, Friedrich Carl von, 150–51

Scaligero, Giulio Cesare, 314

Schack, Adolf Friedrich von, 219–21

Schelling, Friedrich, 25–28, 32, 50, 61, 106, 302, 321

Schelling, Karoline, 25

Schiller, Charlotte von, 92

Schiller, Friedrich, 32, 52, 59, 122, 172, 182, 191, 233, 251, 257, 259, 266, 300–01

Schlegel, Friedrich, 52, 107, 150, 316–17

Schlesier, Gustav, 227, 313

Schmid, Siegfried, 73, 284, 297

Schmidt, Jochen, 100, 297

Schopenhauer, Johanna, 92, 94

Schreiner, Gottlob, 188, 189, 196, 330

Schulze, Johannes, 160, 169

Schwab, C. T. (Christoph Theodor), 22, 234, 249, 252, 256, 258, 263–64, 268, 270–71, 279, 281, 291, 293–94, 312

Schwab, Gustav, 13, 27, 35, 150, 159, 172–74, 191, 198–99, 206, 211, 217, 257, 260, 262, 270, 276, 284, 293

Schwab, Sophie, 255

Schwarz, actor, 120

Seckendorf, Leo von, 62, 103, 107, 121, 126, 155, 217

Seeger, furrier, 267

Seume, Johann Gottfried, 220

Shakespeare, William, 150

Silcher, Philipp Friedrich, 235

Sillaer, Herr von, 194

Sinclair (also Sainclair, St Clair), Isaac von, 22, 28–29, 43, 44, 47–50, 58, 61–65, 68, 73, 79, 81, 83, 87, 89, 105, 107, 121, 127, 134, 148, 159, 208, 247, 260

Socrates, 40

Sommineer, Herr von, 194

Sophocles, 22, 25, 27, 29, 31, 32–34, 37, 40, 70, 115, 117, 119, 170, 232, 269, 282, 284

Soult, Nicolas Jean-de-Dieu, 114

Spinoza, Baruch, 325

Staiger, Emil, 58

Staps, Friedrich, 124

Starobinski, Jean, 313

Stäudlin, Gotthold Friedrich, 164, 191

Stäudlin, Rosine, 203

Strohlin, Jakob Friedrich, 26

Swift, Jonathan, 30

Talleyrand, Charles-Maurice de, 112

Tieck, Ludwig, 107, 150

Uhland, Ludwig, 13, 121, 150, 155, 163, 170–72, 174, 180, 191, 197, 199, 205–06, 211, 217, 271, 279, 293

Varnhagen, Rahel, 145

Varnhagen von Ense, Karl, 115, 131, 197

Villani, Matteo, 6

Vischer, Theodor, 191

Voigt, Christian Gottlob, 80, 92, 96, 100, 116

Voss, Heinrich, 32

Vulpius, Christiane, 90, 122

Wachholder, translator, 115

Waiblinger, Wilhelm, 173–74, 176, 179, 180, 182–85, 187, 189–90, 193–94, 210–11, 257, 259–60, 296, 303

Waldner, Fräulein von, 86

Walser, Robert, 325

Weisser, Friedrich, 101, 103

Wieland, Christoph Martin, 193, 252

Wilhelm of Prussia, Princess (Maria Anna of Hesse-Homburg, Princess), 160, 169

Wilmans, Friedrich, 29, 31

Winckelmann, Johann Joachim, 160

Wintzingerode, Count, 63, 65

Wolzogen, Karoline, 122

Wurm, Christian Friedrich, 174, 177

Zachariae (Zachariä), Justus Friedrich Wilhelm, 232

Zeller, guardian, 264, 268–69, 274, 278, 326

Ziller, Karl, 172

Zimmer, family, 128, 261

INDEX OF NAMES

Zimmer, Christian, 185

Zimmer, Ernst, 10, 30, 105,
109, 132–37, 140, 142,
144, 165–67, 184–86,
199–207, 209, 211–16,
221, 225–28, 230, 235–
44, 271, 293, 326

Zimmer, Lotte, 253, 259,
261, 269, 274, 283, 290,
326

Zimmer, Frau, 158, 228, 265,

Zinkernagel, Franz, 49n25

Zirwizaer, Herr von, 195

Zix, Benjamin, 92

Zollikofer, Georg Joachim,
233

Zwilling, Jacob, 91, 121, 127,
134